Night Driving

Night Driving

the invention of the wheel

& other blues

Dick Dorworth

Western Eye Press

2013

NIGHT DRIVING

is published by Western Eye Press,

a small independent publisher

(very small, and very independent)

with a home base in the Colorado Rockies

and an office in Sedona Arizona,

Night Driving is also available

in various eBook formats.

© 2013 Dick Dorworth

Western Eye Press

P. O. Box 1008

Sedona, Arizona 86339

1 800 333 5178

www.WesternEyePress.com

First Western Eye Press edition, 2013.

ISBN13: 978-0-941283-35-9

First electronic edition, 2013.

ISBN13: 978-0-941283-36-6

Night Driving first appeared in

Mountain Gazette, in February, 1975.

This book is set in

Garamond Premier Pro.

Cover photo by Linde Waidhofer.

FOREWORD TO THE FOREWORD

LITO TEJADA-FLORES

There was a time, it was the late 60s into the 70s. There was a community, well almost a community, loose-knit and far-flung, skiers, climbers, mountain people, the actual dwellers in those funky foothill towns and those still funkier mountain towns trying hard to become respectable ski resorts, and all those would-be mountain folks dreaming of getaways and never quite getting away, from Denver or Sacramento, to follow their hearts into the hills. And there was a forum, a soap box, a kind of town square of a virtual and purely mythical mountain town, a magazine—that magazine was *Mountain Gazette*. Little more than a folded newsprint broadsheet when I first saw it, first dived into stories by some scattered friends who I was surprised could write so well, and writers I wished were my friends, and some mysterious characters whose identities we never did figure out (Who wrote those crazy NED columns, anyway?). *Mountain Gazette* eventually got a nicely printed card-stock cover, with better, almost glossy black and white printing, and a stapled binding, but the newsprint was forever, and so was the austere semi-Bauhaus layout replete with Helvetica press-type heads and zany turn-of-the-century line-art illustrations when there were no Bob Chamberlain photos available... *Mountain Gazette* was a magazine and a half, or so I thought, so we all thought.

And there was one guy, a real and really inspired editor making it all happen, behind the monthly excitement of first-person rants, down-and-out travel tales, and prose poems about life in the West and the mountains of the West, mostly the West, always the West—with a few nods to New England— and all the wide-open spaces between those mountains and those devoted readers and those crazy writers. Michael Moore was the editor, publisher, and layout meister for that original *Mountain Gazette*, gluing down pages with rubber cement in a house-cum-office in downtown Denver, and—although I only met him much later—giving ski bums and dirt-bag climbers with literary ambitions, and river rats who could write, and proto-poets like me, space to spread our wings and say and publish the damnedest things. Things we didn't think anyone would ever publish, but Mike Moore did. It was thrilling. It sure as hell made me think I could be a writer, was a writer. *Hey look: there's my story in Mountain Gazette*. And I know that it worked like that for more than a few mountain scribes. George

Sibley was one, the same George Sibley who wrote that classic Rocky Mountain book, *Part of a Winter*. Dick Dorworth, my skiing guru and sometime climbing partner, was another. And there were many more.

Much of my own best writing appeared first in *Mountain Gazette*, and even after I knew I was a *Mountain Gazette* writer, for real, I felt surprised, tickled, delighted every time my ramblings received Mike Moore's imprimatur. And no surprise, the text of this book, Dick Dorworth's epic *Night Driving*, also appeared first in *Mountain Gazette*. A whole big fat issue of *Mountain Gazette*. An issue still safely racked on an extra-deep shelf in my bookcase along with my whole precious collection of original *Gazettes*. Looking back I realize that Moore was ahead of his time, way ahead of his time. He didn't wait till the digital revolution democratized publishing, he just did it, somehow. No one ever quite knew how. But in our world *Mountain Gazette* made history, was history, our history— history worth reading, reading and re-reading. Let's do it!

—*Lito Tejada-Flores*
Casa Mármol, Patagonia, Chile

FOREWORD

GEORGE SIBLEY

It was a shot from the past, the invitation to write a foreword for Dick Dorworth's *Night Driving*. And it brought a lot of the "past imperfect" back to the present. Dorworth and I have each written a lot for a publication that is kind of iconic in certain marginal circles, Mountain Gazette. We might each have logged more words per person than any other writers for the magazine (with the exception of current Gazette editor John Fayhee, coming up fast on the inside lane). We were both writing for the Gazette before it was Mountain Gazette, when it was called Skiers Gazette, back in the 1960s.

In 1972 Gazette editor Mike Moore—not much of a skier himself —got tired of publishing rambling self-indulgent ski-adventure stories, ski-misadventure stories, rants about the commercialization of skiing, et cetera, and changed the name to Mountain Gazette with the subtitle, "A Magazine Generally About Mountains." Some of Moore's stable of writers continued to write frequently about skiing, but Moore had a very broad (you might say vague) definition of "generally about mountains" which included rambling self-indulgent stories about climbing, floating, hiking, fishing, and just about anything else one might do in the mountains. But he also included rambling self-indulgent reflections from those who had come to the mountains more or less in retreat from the civilization below, and found themselves looking back down the road at that civilization from the higher, clearer perspective the mountains seemed to promise.

Dorworth and I were sort of the apple and orange of that broadly (you might say vaguely) conceived journal. What we probably had in common, based on things that came out in our scribblings, was a developed and accepted awareness that we did not fit very well into mainstream American culture, and had gone to the mountains in the same spirit as rebels, revolutionaries and other banditos have always gone to the mountains. But beyond that common motivation, similarities ended.

Dorworth was, is, an outdoor adventurer. He was a ski racer from his early teens; in 1963 he went to Portillo where he set the world record for speed on skis— probably, when you think about it, the world record for a human moving on land without machine power. He has taught skiing, run ski schools, and coached the U.S. Men's Ski Team; but one gets the sense from his writing about it that he would just as soon be off in the boonies, tree-skiing in unpacked powder up to his neck, or doping out a route up some remote cliff no one else had ever even seen, let alone climbed. He has skied, climbed, hiked and explored the mountains of Europe, Asia and South America, but the mountains of the western U.S.—the Sierras where he grew up and the northern Rockies where he now lives—are the home of his heart.

I, on the other hand, am not an outdoor adventurer. I ski (almost entirely cross-country now) and hike a lot, but I always look for the easier routes up and down the mountains, and when it comes to rivers, I am now (following a promise to God on a trip down the Grand Canyon in which he didn't drown me) completely riparian—I hang out on the banks, and don't even fish. Not, in short, an outdoor adventurer. What came to intrigue me in the mountains are the end-of-the-road towns you find there, and the diverse mix of people they accumulate—all of us challenged and inspired in different ways by the surround of mountains that don't give a damn for us, and all of us working through a lot of baggage from the world below. I tended to write about that—first as a newspaper-man, then as a contributor to any publication that would have me—mainly the Gazette. When not writing for actual dollars, which was most of the time, I worked at whatever would keep a roof overhead and food in a fridge for a growing family—bartender, construction worker, sawyer in a small sawmill, forest-fire fighter, snow-shoveler, et cetera. When someone asked that most American of questions: "What do you do?" I always thought of Zorba's answer: "Do? My hands do the work; who am I to question?"

So that was the two of us, Dorworth and I, both living in the mountains, but in worlds that mostly overlapped only in mountain-town bars, and not always too much, even there. The biggest overlap—sometimes contentious—came in the swirl around available mountain-town women. That was, is, the world of the Mountain Gazette. I've been reading Dorworth for decades, without ever meeting the man in person; nevertheless, I have met a lot of the people he would probably gravitate toward after shaking my hand, if we were ever to meet.

I had a great-uncle who spent "part of a winter" (36 years) in the Colorado mountain town of Silverton, who clarified this split for me. He lived in Silverton back when it was a serious mining town, but with city people already coming up on the train to take pictures, fish and hunt—affording locals a few opportunities to escape the mines if they wanted to, which Uncle Harley did. Like his grand-nephew a few decades later, he was a jack of all trades.

One job he told me about was working as an outfitter for hunters—packing gear in on mules, setting up base camps, pointing the great white hunters in the direction of the elk, et cetera. I observed that he was "a real mountain man." "Oh no," he said, "I'm a valley man." Those high-country camps were the upper edge of his territory; he lived and worked in the valley. That is a valuable distinction, and I think it holds for Dorworth's world versus mine.

So what am I doing writing a foreword to Dick's book?

Well, he asked, for one thing. And even though I have always felt standoffish around "mountain men," I know that I am as far beyond civilization as they are, and as crazy in my own ways. After all, we all live in the virtual bar that is Mountain Gazette by choice. But what made me accept the invitation to write this forward is my personal connection to the story this foreword is supposed to introduce. *Night Driving* first appeared in the winter of 1975 as a long Gazette essay. A really long essay—so long, taking up so much of the magazine that, at first, it pissed me off. But I read it anyway, and it quickly sucked me in (although of course I never told Dorworth) because here was one place where our lives, and our mountain worlds really did overlap, in the long tunnels the headlights carve through the night in an all-night drive—a phenomenon that in itself is a kind of self-induced madness, a stupid thing to do (however necessary) that takes one out of ordinary reality into a parallel universe where your other mind, the one that doesn't mind, wakes up and takes over your wheel.

Dorworth's *Night Driving* is written like one of those coffee-stoked nights. It needs to be read in one sitting, like one of those long nights shared with friends whom Dorworth calls "the brother fuck-ups of the lost highway." Sometimes you will be the guy in the back seat screaming "We gotta slow down!" Sometimes you might drift off in a riff that rolls on like the endless stretch of nightway between Winnemucca and any-where. Sometimes you will be totally charged and energized by the kind of conversation that can only happen when you get tired enough in that jazzed and jangled four ayem way to let it happen. Sometimes you will stop for just a minute to get out of the story and run around madly or do jumping jacks to get the blood flowing again. But jump back in then and finish it: in one sitting.

Night driving. If you're reading this, you have probably been there, and some madness—at ourselves, at the world, or just at the distances between us and our lives—gets us into and through the night and its headlong endless headlight tunnel. Most of us. The brother fuck-ups of the lost highway. Sisters too, in some of my night drives anyway. I remember a Pittsburgh-to-Georgetown (Colorado) straight-through with a woman who had decided, instantly in a bar, to risk her engagement and a job to go skiing by herself for a few days a thousand miles from home. It was nothing to do with me. And my most distinct memory from that trip was waking up in the night on her shift, somewhere on US 36 in Kansas, with her driving 60-70 miles an hour in a snowstorm on a snow-packed road. She scared me so badly that there was nothing to do but go back to sleep and hope it was just a dream.

That episode was part of a period of night driving in my life when I was actually more or less certified as kind of crazy, at least in the opinion of a good-cop-bad-cop team of Army psychiatrists, following a night flight on which I absented my-self without official leave from a society I thought was going crazy. To this day, I don't know if I was actually among the "walking mad" or if I just pulled off a scam on the Army which decided to just ease me out the back door lest I get too noisy. I don't feel a bit more or less sane than I felt then, almost 50 years ago. But there was a definite spurt of night driving, long cross-country hauls between my Pennsylvania past and back to my Colorado future, all in an aging Nash Rambler that finally gave up the ghost on Trout Creek Pass when I was moving my life possessions, which still fit in a Rambler trunk, to Crested Butte and the Upper Gunnison Valley, where I still am. Still crazy, or not, after all these years.

But re-reading *Night Driving* brings it all back, that whole mix of mountain people and valley people in the virtual bar called the Mountain Gazette, where the dusk-to-dawn riders of the night gather to stare or glare across the room at each other, there in the mountains where we all found ourselves. More or less.

And someday, Dorworth, I hope we'll actually meet, in some mountain bar, or even by chance in some clean well-lighted place in the night on the interstates of the soul. See what we really do have to say to each other, if anything, beyond all we've tried to say in the Gazette. Write on.

—*George Sibley*
Gunnison, Colorado

PREFACE

Night Driving was written in an unrelenting, focused burst of energy in three months at the end of 1974. Writing, like skiing and climbing, has always helped keep me on track, particularly in times when the track is icy, rough and hard to see. 1974 was an uncommonly unsettling, unsettled, difficult, confusing and, at the same time, joyous and satisfying time living in Bear Valley, Squaw Valley, Jackson Hole, San Carlos de Bariloche, Yosemite and points in between. Some of those peripatetic times were spent living and traveling around western America in my 1938 Chevrolet pickup with the redwood camper on the back in the company of my three-year-old son, Jason.

Both of us needed a bit more stability, routine, creature comforts and space than life in the old Chevy allowed, so that fall we left the road and moved into a small cabin on Montreal Road between Truckee and Squaw Valley in the Tahoe Sierra where we would live for the next five years. Getting off the road and removing one's hands from the steering wheel opens up a great deal more time, energy and creativity (and hands) for the solitary road of writing. I started out the dynamics of daily (and nightly) life on Montreal Road by writing *Night Driving*, most of it, appropriately enough, written at night. The first draft was written in longhand in a spiral bound 8½-by-11-inch notebook. Then I rewrote it in another notebook and finally transferred it to the typewritten page via my Royal portable typewriter given to me by my father for my 15th birthday and which I used for nearly 40 years until its spirit was broken by the invasion of the computer which banished it to the closet reservation where it passed away of old age.

All writing, particularly the memoir, is or should be at least as mentally, spiritually, and emotionally nutritious to the author as it is to the reader. The process of writing *Night Driving* forced me to delve into events and aspects of my life and times that were richer and more significant than they might appear on the surface. The work of the story teller helps light up the road of life, including long nights of racing from one crisis to another, from one war to another and from one ideology to the next. Telling stories encourages every driver to take it easy and pay attention to the present moment because it contains all the past and determines all the future and is the only moment we really have.

When I had a 100-page manuscript ready I sent it to Mike

Moore, the good editor of *Mountain Gazette*, in hopes that he might see fit to publish it in three or four installments, as most submissions were in the 10-to-20 page range. Mike chose to devote most of the February 1975 issue to *Night Driving*, with a shorter, sterling piece by Ed Abbey, *Desert Driving*, filling up the rest. It was thrilling to have my name on that Bob Chamberlain cover photograph along with one of my literary (and cultural) heroes, Ed Abbey.

Since then *Night Driving* has taken on a life of its own, which is all one can ask of any story ever told by every man, woman and child attempting to light up and stay on the road of civilization and discover what sort of human we are, and why, and how.

N   I   G   H   T

D R I V I N G

A FEW YEARS PAST I visited Ron Funk in his teeny Ketchum condo, figuring to offer whatever comfort and support a man can give an old friend encased in the thirty-seventh cast of his life. Ron, balding and never one to take things lightly, had just had his ankle fused, the culminating therapy for a mining accident which had worked him over several years previously. During our talk that day he said something that lit up a dim section of my brain like the light some say is at the end of one of the tunnels. "Actually," he philosophized, pointing with emphasis to his heavy, white leg with the brown toes sticking out the end, "it's not so bad; one of the things I'm good at is recovering."

Strange talent, to be good at recovering, but no better one to possess for a man who tends to get hurt from time to time.

The thing is, he who often injures himself will, in the perfect wisdom of his own nature, get good at the art of recovery. Isn't excellence only the complete answer to need? The artist learns his skills because his soul requires it, just as the banker learns to count to meet the demands of his soul. To find out who a person is, look to what he does and how well he does it; and there it is possible to discover the individual. There's a reason people are good at what they do. A person good at recovery hurts himself a lot. Skills fit need, need answers skill.

And what bizarre talents all of us cultivate to keep the balance. Salesmanship. Postage-stamp collecting. Endurance. Enduring pain. Rapping. Trapping. Running. Quickness—mind-type, for the others are temporary, therefore, in the later (there is no final) analysis, not so quick. Organization. Logic. Perspicacity. Astuteness. Audacity. And the no-talent is just too much to comprehend. I know a couple of our brothers and sisters whose sole talent is craziness, but they are good at it; being 'crazy' is the means some people use to cop out of keeping their own scene in order, leaving others to pick up after them. And there are others who are good at picking up after the crazies. There are beggars whose talent is to evoke pity, businessmen who know there are few things that can't be bought—and sold. Good professional athletes can tune their bodies as well as Segovia can tune a guitar. Some people have acquired the skill of tapping the energy of the people around them, mixing it with their own considerable stash, using it, working with it and giving it back twofold. I know a few of this type who leave out the last step; but one of these days, in one of the moves of the great cosmic dance of life doing its steps around the grinding wheel of karma, they'll get theirs.

We all have funny little talents we've acquired, developed and polished to cope with the life style/system/scene in which we live. One of mine is night driving. I don't mean just driving a few miles or hours through the night, but real night driving. The dusk-till-dawn patrol. Driving into the darkness of the personal habit of rest, and on through the night to a dawn of numbness, sun-up red eyes, a brightness too real to believe and—the reward—all those miles behind.

I developed into a night driver as a natural consequence of the demands of an early education as ski racer. Long drives into the night in uncomfortable positions in crowded back seats were as real and familiar as Sierra cement, snow blindness, hands thawing after three hours of no feeling, politically-minded little-league ski parents (not mine, fortunately), monstrous ruts, ill-prepared courses and putting on chains before I was old enough to drive—back in the early 50s when the saltiness of Truman gave way to the blandness of Eisenhower and his distasteful vice-president; Stalin dies; the Korean police action ends; Marilyn is both vamp and victim of our society; Hemingway gets the Nobel; Bill Haley rocks around the clock, Bo Diddley diddles the best and Chuck Berry steals the stage, but jazz is still king; James Dean touches a few nerves and unclogs a channel or two; that asshole McCarthy conducts his witch hunts; and my family periodically rises before dawn to watch the atom bombs light up the Nevada horizon of my childhood.

My first influence as a night driver was, not surprisingly, my good father. In the early Lake Tahoe years (1946-52), my mother and father spent their summer months working double shifts in the fabled Nevada casinos and the rest of the year getting by on unemployment and a few moonlight jobs. That was before Tahoe got raped by the greed heads and their flunkies and, since winter tourism didn't exist at Tahoe in those days, an entire subculture of winter unemployables thrived on that work/non-work schedule. Most of those people were coming off the wall of havoc World War II had played with their heads and lives.

I think it was a healthy way for them to live at the time. This existence gave a young ski racer's parents lots of time to get into their son's skiing, and mine did. As a matter of fact, a sub-subculture developed in those days among junior-skier parents in the West which I have never seen rivaled for sheer funk; the equivalent culture of the present junior ski-racing circuit has too much money, too much organization and too much pressure—like the rest of society—and it, too, has some hard, much-needed changes coming around the next bend. My father drove us to all the races. My mother knew how but seldom drove. She hated the automobile, feared it, resented its wheel in her hands, loathed snow on the road and of course she dreaded those times when there was no practical choice but for her to do it herself. Only major family crises enticed her into an airplane, and her unhappiness on those occasions would have been funny was it not so real. I think now she may have been listening to a primordial wisdom deeper than the fear of bodily death we thought was at the root of it. She knew something unnatural and suspect lurked about engines and combustion noise and anything moving faster than a gallop.

My father, however, took to the automobile just like Henry Ford knew he would. After an initial fascination with the upper reaches of the beast's potential for velocity, which inevitably ended with a couple of demolished vehicles and some perspectives on life he hadn't considered previously, my father slowed down and became devoted to the automobile as a rational tool of transportation instead of a rushing ride on his ego. By the time I was old enough to remember driving with him he had reached the latter stage. As I grew into my teens, and, alas, out of them, quite naturally my father's driving drove me up the wall. Any young fool could see that he wasn't using his machine's maximum potential. I remember spending three days and two nights on awful roads with him guiding six of us from Reno to Whitefish, Montana, for a ski race. He drove through at least one night because I insisted we'd never get there should he stop, but I was so blown out and nervous and up tight that I drove home with some lead foots after the races. Father—such was his style—took five days to drive back, and as he described it, "had a wonderful time." He drove me many a night through the night into the hours where muscles ache and nerves are numb and eyes cannot be believed, but he never hurt a human being with a car.

My next influences in the subtle art of ignoring the gentle rhythms of sun and moon, blasting along the night whiteline-whitelinewhitelinewhitelinewhiteline highways of America were my friends, my coaches and a few assorted parents. Friends: Bob and Warren Lerude, Bud Sorenson, Lynn Johnson, Howie Norton. Coaches: Dick Munn, Hal Codding, Joe Auckenthaler (Gordy Wren was the best ski coach I knew as a boy, but he was never a driving influence). Assorted parents: Milt and Renee Zimmerman and 'Tank' Smith more than anyone else.

The first introduction to Sun Valley, still my favorite place to ski, was after an all-nighter. Bob Lerude, Bud Sorenson and I made the journey from Reno, starting after high school classes in March 1953, in a pick-up with a prehistoric camper on the back. Bob's father, Les, was a well-known Reno restaurateur, specializing in hot apple pie; and on the front and sides of his silver camper he had painted hot apple P*I*E with the P*I*E in red, like the big P*I*E trucks that transported America's wares around America's roads in those long-ago miles, and nearly every P*I*E truck we passed honked at us. That was Les' idea of a good joke, and we enjoyed it too. Bob did all the driving, and

I stayed up all night rapping to keep him company, Bud asleep in the back.

That's one way to make it through—talking. Sometimes it works, but other times the all-night driver gets into his own head trip and any interference makes him a distracted driver. When it works, the extended all-night driving rap is a sign of high sympathetic communion between participants. It is well known that lack of sleep breaks down defenses, destroys the ego, and separates the person from his body (he falls asleep at the wheel otherwise), all of which combine to enable interested minds to interact without some of the usual obstacles thrown up by ego, weird hang-ups and bad past experiences which create the defensive mind. We all know other means to the same end, but talking through the night with another human is admirable relief for the unremitting, lost loneliness of the long-distance driver, a loneliness deeper, wider and blacker than the casual thinker might think; a loneliness going beyond the fact of driving through the endless night when more-together brothers and sisters are warmly asleep in each other's arms; yes, past that fact into the reasons why a person winds up with a cold steering wheel in his hands instead of a warm woman, fatigue in his body and a destination-goal in his mind outside the perfect present, which is only perfect if loneliness is perfect, and—O my sweet plastic Jesus of the dashboard—it isn't.

We pulled into Sun Valley on that long-ago March night a couple of hours before dawn and crashed in the back of the truck. When we woke, chalky mouthed, fiery-eyed and achy-boned, we crawled out of the camper into a perfect Sun Valley day. The first thing we saw was the 1953 moguls on Exhibition, the most beautiful, exciting sight I'd ever seen. It was love at first vision, me and Bald Mountain, a long-standing love affair that persists to this day, unlike, alas, some others there have been along the road. In a manner that must be felt and sensed rather than explained, riding the narrow, all-night 1953 Nevada and Idaho highways of the mind, in open conversation with my boyhood friend, Bob Lerude, helped prepare me to recognize on sight the finest skiing mountain in America. As a skier, that was an important moment in life. It was an instant akin to that when a guitarist first hears a Martin, a climber see the Cerro Torre close up, a feared drug addict lays eyes on eighty acres of his favorite cannabis sativa blowing in the mind, and that magical (mythical?) (myriad?) realization that blinds the heart and mind and sex of every person at encountering for the first time the love that will never die, the kiss that will never cool. The second time is, altogether, re-affirmation, mind-bender, faith-healer and heart-stomper. The third time is pure faith. After that, it is so far out on the edge that only those who have been there know the precarious balance—tightrope walking a thread above the first and last and only abyss—involved in going for it again, once again, along America's endless highways that go nowhere, end nowhere, begin nowhere and circle continually inward in a seemingly endless spiral toward the self that should love and must be love and can be nothing else and is—love—lost along the passageways of the fiery human heart encased in the crazy human frame blasting down the eternal concrete/asphalt cables with which we have bound together this beautiful land called America which must someday burst its bonds the way only love—pure, unadulterated, simple love—can.

ANOTHER WAY THROUGH THE LONG HIGHWAY NIGHT that I learned before I was old enough to drive is with the aid of the drug, alcohol, in the form of beer for the most part, wine sometimes. My first cohort and strongest early influence in the crass, jagged art of multi-houred drunk driving was Warren Lerude, Bob's younger brother, one year my senior, who owned an out-a-sight Chevy sedan that took us many happy places and saw us explore the entire range of experience, philosophy, joy, sorrow, love and heartbreak available to high-energy, precocious teenagers of the mid-1950s. Warren and I drank our way together down uncountable roads, through many a night, past unbearable teenage crises and over the necessary mountains of that time. Warren gave up the midnight shift at the wheel for the alternative and became an editor and publisher for the newspaper in Reno and then a journalism professor at the University, and he won a Pulitzer along the way. It's hard on the road but it has its compensations, as, of course, does being off the road; and everybody must choose what they can live with, or, rather, without.

Warren and I once made a night run to Redding, California, for a high school football game. We were so blitzed we scared ourselves sober and then tucked away our rational fear into another case of Falstaff, laughing like crazy at the world speeding by outside the windows, a world purposely dimly perceived and as little as possible felt from inside the Chevy cubicle—our one space which a non-understanding, hostile, hypocritical adult world could not reach. The automobile freed an entire generation of Americans, if you accept the premise that generations are not determined by age, but rather, by mentality; or, there are no generation gaps, only mind gaps. The car was our bedroom, bar, forum, transportation, kicks (I once played bumper tag at 115 mph, and when the highway patrolman finally caught us, between Mammoth and Lee Vining, he was really upset; but, luckily, my tag partner was the Lee Vining ski team coach—a responsible adult—and the next door neighbor of the patrolman who couldn't really believe us, but he let us off. I've known a lot of luck like that) and solace.

The car radio gave us Elvis with his liberating sounds, and the back seat allowed us to blunder in privacy and security into the astounding, forbidden, lied-about, fabled, dangerous, wonderful world of sex. And sex can be used for many purposes—liberation, loving, healing, expression, betrayal, entrapment, pleasure, ego-gratification, comfort, learning and it is even used by the jaded for getting off on pain. We learned first to let sex liberate us, sweet liberation. But we move slightly out of night driving. The mind wanders, like a restless gypsy.

One of my hardest early journeys—again with Warren—covered a span of about two weeks, and took us from Reno to Provo, Utah, to Alta to Sun Valley and back to Reno. All driving was accompanied by cold beer; we never commenced driving before 10 p.m.; we skied every day and raced a few in Sun Valley. On our third leg of the journey, Jim Gilbert had a terrible time, much to his dread and our amusement. Jim, who was killed two years later in a car wreck, was honest, intelligent, hard working, non-boozing and terrified of our entire show. I remember the saying, "Only the good die young." Warren and I rode in front with a case of beer between us. Jim sat in back, his chin resting on the front seat, watching our every move, advising, commenting, trying to slow down, shut down, come down on our entire scene; but, at the same time, somewhat fascinated by it without ever, ever wanting involvement in it any deeper than as a participant/observer with his life at stake.

The last stage of that journey is typical of the whole gig of piloting automobiles through the night with beer as protein for the body, alcohol as vitamin for the mind. We partied in Sun Valley until midnight after the races; then we loaded up the car with skis, luggage, Gilbert and enough beer and food for the twelve hours it would take to get to Reno in those days. We had no spare tire, two bald ones, and not enough money to buy anything but beer and gas. Our original solution was to heist some tires off a car in the Sun Valley parking lot. We were wandering around the midnight rows of cars, carrying jack and lug wrench, checking out the prospects, when the Sun Valley detective emerged from the ether.

"What're you boys doing at this time of night?" he asks.

"Oh, nothin,'" Warren answers, twiddling the lug wrench like Captain Queeg playing with his ball bearings, and the jack in my hands feels like a day-glo bazooka in black light. "Just getting our car packed, cause we're leaving town. We're just looking for the car now." The detective looked at us a long time—fifteen and sixteen years old and both drunk—and declared, "Okay, but you'd better get going."

We solved the problem in Twin Falls by touring the darkest, quietest, early-morning streets until we found a car with the appropriate-sized tires, jacked it up, removed two, laid it gently down upon its axle, and took the fastest route out of town. During this entire escapade, from its inception during packing, while Warren and I discussed logistics, until we were laughing our way away from Twin Falls, Jim tried his hardest to talk us out of it with a sincerity born of an honest man's dread of thievery, and, of course, getting caught. As it turned out, the bald tires held up the whole way; but there was no way to know that in advance; and you gotta cover yourself unless you want to get stranded sometime in a Nevada desert and I don't, though there are, in the long run, easier ways to cover yourself. The karma of theft comes down as hard as any other kind, and that, as any brother fuckup of the road who has experienced the tap-tap-tap of God's hammer upon his being knows, is very hard indeed.

We careened along the Idaho/Nevada desert night, through Contact, Wells, Elko, Battle Mountain, Winnemucca—drinking, eating, pissing, laughing and talking our way into some of the first, full-on but faltering steps toward knowing ourselves—and sometime in the morning, after the harsh sun had turned the just-dark land into a glaring sea of changing desert colors, which brought out the shades, we gave our friend Jim Gilbert his worst moments of the trip.

Somewhere around Lovelock we emptied the last glass bottle of the case we front-seaters had between us. At this point we had been driving for about ten hours, drinking for eighteen and awake for nearly thirty; and our fifteen and sixteen-year-old minds must have seemed pretty strange to our back-seat friend, completely sober and the elder at seventeen.

We called to the back for the second case of beer. Jim didn't like that at all, but he eventually passed it over. This presented us with more than fifty bottles in the front seat, since there had been a few beers besides the cases, half of them empty. A crowded situation. Warren, blonde and chubby, with an uncombed flattop, saddle shoes, Levis and a T-shirt, peered silently through chic prescription shades into his own endless highway, puffing on the constant cigarette of his habit. As the driver he had the heaviest responsibility, and it takes a lot of concentration to destroy yourself and still keep things on the road. No company there at the moment. Gilbert, trustworthy and a friend, was on an entirely different track.

What to do? What to do? What to do with yourself and a front seat full of empty bottles when you're fifteen years old and blasted out of your brains and barreling down the great American highways of being a teenager in the 1950s when you know—even though you are on your way back to your boyhood home—you know because you can feel you are going to spend long, hard miles on those endlessly lost asphalt paths that appear to lead everywhere but end nowhere and answer nothing because there is no time to change on that lost highway taken by the human mind sighting down a hood ornament at a world moving by so fast it can only be aimed along, never perceived or touched or felt or merged with or learned from. Even at fifteen, you know there are a lot of dues to pay on the roads of America and the rest of the Earth before the last key is inserted in the last ignition and turned on for the last, last time.

What to do? Zounds! Mercedes Myladies! It was so simple. I rolled down the window, and the green sagebrush air of April Nevada entered the car like a refreshing shot of future nostalgia, clear, full of smells of the land we moved over too fast to know and evoking an innocence lost so long ago that only a sharp sorrow of memory-feeling, as old as the sun on the morning swamp, recalls the ancient dream of the state of innocence. What is it? Where is it? How do we get back to it? Where did it go?

Right out the window with the first empty bottle I aimed at the first road sign I saw. A clean miss. "Shit."

"Hey," Jim protests, "you can't do that."

"Who says?" I say.

"Hey, c'mon, quit doing that."

I had another in my hand, ready to toss. Warren, a loyal and understanding friend, then and now, unlocks himself from the road, peers over at me and gives out a funny grin. Coming up is a road sign on the other side of the 1954 two-lane blacktop, and, since no other cars were in sight, he takes a puff off his eternal cigarette, holds it, lets the smoke out in a stinking cloud and heads into the other lane at 60 mph so I can get a good shot at the sign.

"Oooooooooooo, hey! shit, you guys, hey, c'mon, Warren, get back in the right lane. Hey. Ooooooooo. Hey. This isn't funny," Jim complains.

"On the contrary, Jim, it's funniernshit," I say, climbing out the window so I can get a good shot over the top of the car, laughing deep gut guffaws at all of us at the same time. I took careful aim at the back side of that pillar of direction in the desert and fired away, holding on for all I'm worth to the top inside of the door. A direct hit. The bottle ricocheted off the sign high in the air, and tumbled off through the state flower of Nevada, end over end, like a ground-kicked football. It didn't break.

"Did you see that?" I yelled, "It didn't break." The air rushed by my nearly deafened ears like rapid water over a log, and it was exhilarating.

"Here, try another," Lerude yells, handing me another empty and getting back in the right lane to avoid a bit of startled oncoming traffic.

I took it and held on and waited for the next onrushing target, which I missed. Again, the bottle skittered off through the sagebrush without breaking. I tried another. And another. And another. After about ten throws—Gilbert in the back yelling and complaining and, I'm sure, wondering what he'd ever done to deserve being imprisoned in this traveling looney bin—I observe that only one in three bottles break, a slightly better percentage than my connection with target average, and I grow weary of this game. They don't-make bottles like they used to.

"What're ya' doin'?" Warren asks as I return to the seat.

"You guys are crazy," Jim adds.

"Aw, I'm tired of that," I say.

"What're we going to do with all these empties?" Warren asks, a one-sided grin with a smoky cigarette sticking out, one end of it covering his face

Well, that was when Jim had his hardest moment. Not wasting time talking about it, Warren and I knew what we had to do, as good friends tend to know together the next step, and Jim knew what we were going to do too. I began loading all the stray bottles into the cardboard case of empties. Jim saw immediately what was up.

"O no, O no, O no you don't, you crazy bastards," he said, reaching across the seat, trying to grab the case. I was forced to the violent extreme of beating him back, wrestling with him for the case, me laughing and him yelling the whole time. Warren starts making swerves with the car, running slalom with every twenty-fifth piece of white line. There we are—Warren and me laughing and enormously enjoying ourselves, Jim yelling like crazy and wrestling with me for the case of empties, the whole time freaked out of his mind, and the car careening back and forth across the Nevada highway. Finally, I won the case from Jim, and shoved it through the window. Since we happened to be in the wrong lane at that moment, the case landed right in the middle of the road. It shattered in a thousand pieces in a huge explosion, and it looked as if not a bottle had survived. (Never could understand that one.) Pieces of glass and cardboard were strewn all over the highway, and I'm sure we picked up the karma of more than one flat tire during the next few days.

"You assholes, you assholes," Gilbert kept saying.

We only laughed and had another beer. We got to Reno and took Jim home, and he had cooled out by then. He thanked us for a fine trip, and said he'd had a wonderful time. The three of us laughed, but I know he meant his words. It is sometimes healthy for a person who won't gross himself out to have other less sensitive souls do it for him. I mean the gross-out has a beneficial side, just like taking a shit is a good thing to do from time to time; the trick is to pay attention to what kind of food you eat, and how much. Two years later, after his death, Jim's mother told me that our trip together was one of his best memories, and he talked about it often. Strange the things that teaches us in our lives.

After Warren got out of high school a year later I never did much long distance driving behind alcohol. It was a phase best left behind. While alcohol has accompanied many brothers and sisters along the everlasting dark nights of their highway souls, they push a little less hard without a steering wheel in their hands.

SPEAKING OF DRUGS AND THE DRIVE—while alcohol is (as any highway statistic, patrolman or ambulance attendant can verify) the most popular and dangerous mind lubricant on the road, it is by no means the only one in common use. After alcohol, the first one the nighttime long-distance driver learns about is caffeine, usually in the form of terrible, watery, sleazy coffee-shop coffee from the all-night truck stops which, oasis-like, light up the nighttime highways of America at least every hundred miles. America is littered with caffeine addicts who have no idea, and who would be horrified, violent, and even murderous to be told that they, too, are dreaded drug addicts.

Not me. I've been a drug addict for as long as I can remember. Not always peaceable; but, at least, honestly. Caffeine was the first of a series, and that started when I was eleven or twelve, I forget which. Like most things learned by young people, I picked up the caffeine habit from the people I loved and trusted the most—my parents. They were, when I was young, heavy caffeine, nicotine and alcohol users; and, as a matter of fact, excessive nicotine, the only one I never got into, finally destroyed my mother's lungs and killed her the slow, hard way. My first caffeine came in the form of half-coffee half-milk with a healthy dose of white sugar. A little milk and sugar to hide the truth of the matter. A classic beginning and one I have given much thought to.

In those young years of life and skiing I used to rise before Zephyr Cove dawn, on the eastern shore of a relatively unscarred, beautiful, childhood Lake Tahoe, make myself breakfast and a bag lunch, brew a pot of coffee, drink a lot of it, pour some in a Thermos and catch a ride with one of the lift operators to White Hills, that wonderful place of my first skiing at the Spooner Summit junction, connecting South Shore, North Shore and Carson City. I was the first on the lift, the last off, and skied all day with an enthusiasm only available to a twelve-year-old in love with skiing and needing badly to learn. At lunch I drank my Thermos of coffee, and it is little wonder that my undeveloped system had so much energy to devote to skiing. A strong memory of the time is returning home to find my mother furious because I had forgotten to turn off her cherished percolator when I'd left that morning. The machine was burnt to a crisp on the inside and it made a deep enough impression that my mother still told the story nearly twenty years later, not long before she died from another one of her habits. And I guess the impression stuck because when she awoke that morning she was unable to feed her caffeine habit in the manner to which she had become accustomed: there is no greater shock to the system than going cold turkey. Like any enterprising addict, my mother invented her own sheepherder's coffee on the spot; and she kept herself from flipping out, at least until I returned from a day of skiing to be confronted with the charred coffeepot of my negligence.

From such innocuous beginnings, the caffeine habit became a way of life. Before I was fourteen, I had dropped the deceiving milk and sugar from the acrid, true, black coffee which I drink to this day, with great pleasure and shaking fingers. I have been in and out of coffee many times, and once I went more than a year without so much as a sip. The worst it ever got was during my wastrel years as a university student, graduate student and teacher. During the years I was involved with the largest babysitting, mind-fucking service ever known to western man—I mean the American system of university education—I was good for twenty-five or thirty cups of coffee per day.

No wonder, then, that caffeine became the most reliable driving drug for those on the lost, displaced roads of the inverted, moonlight cycle that has been a part of the Americas since Leif Ericson, Chris Columbus, the Pilgrims and Cortez could not bear to be where they were; and who, because they would not take that care we all know must, ultimately, be taken with their lives, places and spaces, were forced out onto the long, watery via perdido in their particular time of lonely adventure, setting down the ground rules for how we would live upon this wonderful land that stretches and sprawls and is, at the same time, interlaced with as many highways as there are blood vessels in the human brain, from Tierra del Fuego to the oil-rich, doomed North Slope of Alaska.

In the mid and late 1950s caffeine was the stimulant which took me through dozens of nights—Seattle to Reno, Aspen to Reno, Sun Valley to Reno, Aspen to Hanover, Salt Lake City to Reno and many others. Funny how so many of the all-nighters were invested in going home, as if only the impetus of that magic word and place and concept—HOME—could force a man to push through his own limitations and habits to the edge. The edge has its hardships, but at least one can be sure that it is life out there (here?) and not the Barbie-Doll, TV-dinner mentality that plasticland has ramrodded down the gullets of those hordes of iron bellies who can stomach Styrofoam horseshit for dinner, breakfast, lunch, brunch, snacks, feasts celebrations and sacrifice.

Home. Where is it? What is it? Where the heart is? The head? The body? Somehow I think of a beautiful expatriate American man who lives in Heidelberg, Germany. Rex Gribble fought in World War II, has-been around every block in the neighborhood at least three times, forsook the U.S. of A. not long after that war, is one of my favorite people and sums up his philosophy thusly: "Life is like a baseball player rounding third base on the way to home, legs pumping like mad, cleats tearing up the dirt, hair flying in the wind because he's pushing so hard his hat fell off—and home plate isn't there."

Ahhhhhhhh. Home plate isn't there. Well, shit. If home plate isn't there, if it has gone the way of Ixtlan and innocence, then what drives us to drive through the night to a home? We keep leaving home in search of—what? Adventure? Amusement? Agreement? America? Is home there when we return? Thomas Wolfe told us you can't go home again, and that's true. And who doesn't know it? Old Chris Columbus knew it. Darwin knew it. Marilyn Monroe knew it. And Don Juan knows it. Ed Mitchell knows it. He has been further out there than anyone, and he came all the way back to earth from the dark side of the moon searching to find home in Noetics. Me and my brother fuck-ups of the lost highway keep repeating those long drives through the night heading for that mythical home our imaginations have placed out there in the future, that home which we have always left in a full-throttle search for whatever is down the road, around the next turn, over the next hill, at the end of the next long straightaway. What is it that the long-distance driver and all other explorers suspect can be found somewhere else but where they are?

The why of the long-distance-night-driver is beyond me,

just as the concept of 'more perfect' becomes meaningless in the face of the destruction of perfection wrought by its pursuit; but it is an ancient tradition that was old before it came to America; its roots are deep and go all the way back to the roots of an apple tree in the Garden of Eden.

So it was caffeine in those days. Coffee and NoDoz. I don't know if NoDoz contains any chemical beside caffeine that would stimulate tired nerves to alertness, but I do know that the taste of NoDoz would make a sedated banana-slug gasp for air like a drowning man coming up for the second time. The taste alone of NoDoz keeps a man from enjoying anything, even sleep; it is so foul that any person who could sleep after eating some would dream of sulfurous acid, the River Styx and all the tormented souls along its banks, volcanoes and sludge and sewage in the streets. It's awful, but in its own way appropriate to night driving.

Actually, when a person is putting terrible substances into his body and brain, and doing hard, gruesome things to himself, he's probably ready to sit down in solitude and silence and take a close look at himself. But so few ever take the time and care to do that. In 1958, when alcohol, NoDoz and coffee were the drugs of our lives, we had a ski race in Ogden, Utah. It was the National Championships, and it had been a hard week. Two people were killed in avalanches; one of them, Tony Deane from Aspen, was one of the racers and a friend to many of us. It snowed all week in classic Utah style. The courses were soft. The downhill had to be shortened. And, more to the point of my own ego time, I had only one respectable result in three races. There were unbelievable political hassles. It was a hard, strange week filled with the taste of Tony's death, and when it was over, everybody came loose. We had an incredible party. (I can still recall the unique, idealistic, crazy Gardner Smith dancing to "Tequila" and giving out coyote yells at irregular intervals.) Around one in the morning—all of us full of tequila, beer and fatigue—we loaded up the car and hit the road. My car mates Cathy Zimmerman, Mary Ann Tonini (who nearly seventeen years later is my landlady at the little cabin near Truckee as I write these lines, and lives with her old man and two kids a hundred feet away), Bunny Rakow and Bud Sorenson immediately fell into comas. I gobbled NoDoz and coffee as if life itself depended on it, cranked Milt Zimmerman's enormous station wagon up to about 110 mph and blasted into the Utah/Nevada night of those perfect high-speed highways, unlike any others in the world. I consumed three or four boxes of NoDoz and just as many Thermos bottles of coffee—just as the vehicle drank more gasoline than I could believe, and for exactly the same reasons.

We finally roared into the amazing and unique little community of Reno, Nevada, America, that mountain/desert/Neanderthal town halfway between reality and fantasy, whose karma and economy and mentality are built upon and sustained by the gambler, that sad soul who has always sacrificed truth to the lost lie of the dice; the man and woman of quick marriage, those careless couples without the patience of a three-day blood-test wait, who flock to Nevada's plastic, obscene wedding chapels and its even more obscene Justices of the Peace who grow rich on marriage fees charged thousands of poor slobs drunk out of their minds on alcohol, emotion, hope, sex and, sometimes, love; the twenty-four-hour bar, to accommodate the out-of-control drinker and other lonelinesses; and divorce, that institution of sorrow belonging to those displaced persons who flock to Reno and Tahoe and Las Vegas like refugees from a war zone, carrying the trashed remainder of their shattered hearts and crushed dreams and broken lives in a bundle on the end of the skinny stick of their humbled pride, the way hobos pass through town on their way from nowhere to nowhere else. Yes, Nevada. Pat Nixon was born in Nevada. It is, truly, God's truth. Yes, Reno. The Chamber of Commerce calls Reno *The Biggest Little City in the World*. The Chamber of Consciousness would call it *The City of Human Weakness and Folly*.

After all I'd done to my system we roared into Reno late in the morning, unable to inflict anything more on the body. Without a wink of sleep, I made all my afternoon classes that day at the University of Nevada school for wastrels, cogs, wheels, screws, nuts, bolts and other parts of the great American establishment machine that grinds up human life the same way Milt Zimmerman's station wagon drank gasoline, and with as much feeling. That's how we lived in those days.

MY FIRST MULTI-DAY NON-STOP DRIVE happened in 1959, probably the last year I ever ingested NoDoz into myself. We had been racing the circuit in the east and when the season was over, we decided to return west. The crew that came together for that drive was an interesting conglomerate of skiers of the time.

Redmond Wilcox owned the car, a new 1959 gas-gobbling Oldsmobile that was good for a solid 120 mph at 5 mpg. Red was a guy you never, ever forgot, once you saw him. He was tall and lean and crew-cut, and he had a wide, red scar that started above hairline, ran down across his forehead, right through his left eyelid, and down across his left cheek. The scar pulled the lower eyelid completely down, exposing the white of his left eye like the most sanpaku window in the history of disharmony. I never did get it straight how he earned that scar, but he made Boris Karloff look like a Sunday school teacher played by Liberace. Not surprisingly, he had some hang-ups the rest of us didn't share. We spent a lot of time with Wilcox that year, and he was a good companion. An Easterner, he was really restless and wanted to go west only in response to that feeling. After the drive, he hung around Reno awhile; and then one day he split, with no farewells, and no one I know ever heard from him again. Too bad. He owes me $50.

Gardner Smith is unique as they come. One of the finest

skiers of the 1950s, he won the Roch Cup in 1958. Gardner was (still was the last time I saw him, in 1968) eccentric, intensely individual, obsessed with the style of things, opinionated, a genius, alienated from the mainstream and, you know, a brother fuck-up of the lost highway. When I was in high school in Reno, Gardner was going to the University of Nevada, and he was easily the best skier in town. I spent a lot of formative time with Gardner—skiing, racing, traveling, drinking, talking, questioning and learning. He was a strong influence on everybody he opened up to, and I was no exception. A couple of days before we started west, Gardner had finished his amateur skiing career with an excellent slalom at Wildcat, New Hampshire; he was pushing thirty and was one of those men who is never going to make it in any but the loosest, most broad-minded, strangest fringe societies of human beings on planet Earth. So it was a turning-point time for Gardner Smith as we started that trip, one of those heavy, changing periods, when a person begins to become another person. Gardner was changing from ski racer to wanderer and he is, God willing, wandering around somewhere to this day having many amazing and crazy adventures of the road.

Don Brooks is the hardest-working, most intense person, in his own way, I've ever known. In those days Brooks was another hacker on the circuit, with less money than most—and more determination. He later became a member of the U.S. National Ski Team, the Denver University ski team, and the 1966 FIS ski team. After he quit racing he organized, coached and financed the Bear Valley and Aspen Wildcat race teams in the late 1960s. A lot of people in skiing owe him a lot. It seems appropriate to remind some people of Brooks' contribution at this time. Don, small and compact with blue eyes, blonde hair and a misleading, innocent smile and baby face, suffered, like many iron-willed self-drivers, from a tendency to push just a little too hard. That's why he spent a few years living on the lam, with a federal indictment or two and a host of Feds on his ass. When he finally finished college he set himself a goal of ten years to make a million dollars. He went for it, as all his friends knew he would. A bit too firmly it turns out. I didn't see him for a few years while he went into the undergrounders underground, but I know he roared around the endless, lost highways of this world in the fastest automobile he could muster and pushed the cops-and-robbers game just as far as it can be pushed. Later he found Jesus, came out of the underground, paid his debt to society, became a businessman, married a woman who loved him dearly, and continued to ski race with grim determination until he dropped dead of a heart attack at dinner some 40 years later.

Renee Cox was the stabilizing female element on that trip. She was the only one among our group the American mainstream of society would term 'normal'. Not that she was 'average', because she was and is an exceptional person; but she possessed the values, goals and judgment that allowed her to fit into a social structure the rest of us only bounce off whenever we get too close to it. Renee was one of the best U.S. racers of the time. A year later she finished in the top ten at the Squaw Valley Olympic slalom. She abandoned racing after that to marry Dave Gorsuch, another Olympic skier. Today the Gorsuchs own Vail's most successful ski shop, raise kids, swim in the mainstream and are, in my opinion, really good folks.

After the races in New Hampshire, we had a magnificent end-of-the season party, and I remember someone crashing into Bill Beck, the Olympic team coach at the time who was on crutches with a broken ankle. The season was finished and the serious racing for the 1950s had ended. For some like Gardner racing itself was ending, and that is an important time in a ski racer's life. There was nothing left to do but get on the highway and get on with something else, even if it was just moving down the road.

First we had to drive to upstate New York. There was no hurry for anyone to be anywhere, and we hung around New York for a day and talked about a leisurely trip west with lots of stops and visiting and sightseeing. Finally, late one morning, we found ourselves ready and with no reason not to leave, so we did.

Our first planned stop was Niagara Falls. Everybody has heard of the big waters and since we were going right by we figured to check them out. But a strange thing happened when we got to the turn-off for Niagara: it was unanimously and spontaneously agreed upon that we should keep going. Suddenly the road itself became more important than anything along the way. We were heading 'home', wherever that is, like horses to the barn, and nothing so puny as Niagara Falls was going to cloud our vision of the bucket of oats. It was a sign we barely noticed. After all, who wants to see Niagara Falls? It's just a lot of water falling off a cliff. "Big deal," we said, and drove on. Several years later I saw Niagara. I was impressed. Especially impressive were the stories of the super-flashes who have gone off the falls in barrels, boats and sundry contraptions, and of one little boy who went over by accident with only a life preserver, and lived.

We drove right up against the speed limits and a little bit past at all times. When it looked good we pushed a long way past. The big, black Olds really had power. It could hit a hundred without trying and the heavy beast felt solid as a tank at any speed, the ideal machine for the cops-and-speeders game we all loved to play.

Renee never drove. I can't think why now, but it must have been the chauvinistic training from which we all suffered. The rest of us took turns, changeover determined by driver's fatigue and/or boredom. We roared through the day and into the night and we stopped to eat, to gas up and to get coffee in the Thermos. Sometime that first night—late and somewhere in Illinois or Indiana—Brooks pushed too hard and missed a cue and got busted for doing 100 in a 75-mph zone. The cop was unhappy, surly and uncooperative and delighted to have us passing through. He was very clever, for we never did figure out where he came from. He must have had an underground tunnel by the freeway. At any rate, he wasn't letting us go with a ticket. So we followed him along the late-night streets of some sleeping little town to the judge's house. He woke the judge who listened to the story in his bathrobe, and then the judge fined Brooks more than he had. Don borrowed some money from me, as I was wealthy at the time. He gave the money to the judge, who, I assume, split it with the pig and returned to bed. The policeman thanked us and went back to seek another score. We hit the road, aware by then that we were going to drive through the night, which we did.

Dawn was memorable for one thing: just after morning light revealed those few bits of the earth not buried beneath asphalt, concrete and steel, we rolled into the outskirts of Chicago, a place that speaks for itself. We felt the way five people do in a two-seat car the morning after they have driven entirely through an American night, pushed—too hard, too fast—with not enough rest, encountered the American judicial system and been welcomed into a new day by Chicago. "Good morning, night dwellers of the lovely, fantasy-planet Earth, which inhabitants of the imagination call paradise. This is Reality. We call it Chicago in these parts, welcoming you to the stockyards, slums, Richard Daley, Judge Julius Hoffmann, Al Capone, a Great Lake of shit and garbage, rampant racism and the Chicago blues." Just then, full of the all-night, early-morning Chicago blues, just becoming aware—once again—of how far it really is to the West Coast, we saw a huge, United Air Lines billboard squeezed in among the seven hundred thirty-six others along that section of the road. The illustration was a bad painting of the hills and buildings and streetcars and Golden Gate Bridge and bay of San Francisco and it said: "San Francisco in five hours with United." (Planes were all propeller-driven in those days.) We knew where we were going to be in five hours—somewhere along the rolling, monotonous highways of Illinois or Missouri, numb, cramped and tired and a long, long way from anything even remotely approaching that magic word, 'home'. That was one of the low points of the trip. I wanted to sell the car right then, buy us all plane tickets to wherever we wanted to go. I explained that he'd have plenty of money left over, but Red wouldn't go for that one.

The second day is a haze. Farmland and rolling, straight, two-lane roads at 100 mph. Cresting each rise was an adrenaline high (you never knew when one of those farmers would be creeping along at 5 mph just over the top in a tractor or thresher or barely moving flatbed loaded with hay). We ate dinner in some tiny town in Kansas just after dark of the second night. We talked about all the people we knew in Denver, and all the things we could do there, and places to stay and rest and be and laugh about. After dinner we headed for Denver with a vague idea of spending a few days there.

The first snow found us a hundred miles east of the Mile High City. By the time we pulled into town in the early hours of a blizzarding day there was nearly a foot of unexpected snow on the springtime streets of Denver. We were all exhausted, and the couple of hours of snow driving—staring through the hypnotic whirl of individual snowflakes, caught during the moment of passing in the headlight glare, using all faculties to see the road through the swirl and keep the beast on it—didn't do us any good. We needed rest, wanted rest, and had thoroughly discussed it, but as we pulled into Denver the same thing that had happened as we passed Niagara happened again. The snow had something to do with it. We were tired of snow and the circuit and skiing, and it was spring and there was sunshine in California. Gardner, the sole California native (if any white man can, in honesty, be called 'native'), was the only one who didn't want to continue.

"Hey, man, let's trade this traveling motel room in on one with a shower and some sheets," he said. But we out-maneuvered, out-pressured and out-numbered him. Onward! Forward! Step on it! Excelsior!

We left Renee, who was staying in Denver to go to school, at a motel. We got her settled into a Colfax classic, said our farewells, and headed into the wet blizzard with a certain loss at leaving behind one of the group and a certain relief at having the extra space in the car. It was Gardner's turn at the wheel, but he gave in to fatigue and the bad grapes all of us exhibit when we are out-voted and being pushed by others beyond what we feel like pushing. I took the wheel, and the rest of the car was asleep before I skidded out of Denver. I ate NoDoz and sucked coffee and listened to Wolfman Jack on the radio and peered into the monotonous hypnotoscope of headlight snow. I put myself in tune with the system, in order to keep the great black beast on the path. There was no task in the universe superior to keeping our vehicle on the road, and in a certain sense there could be no better training for life than taking the beast and your friends' lives in your own hands, and guiding them through the slippery, snowy, tired night without succumbing to the loneliness of the long-distance driver and wrecking everything, the way those careless souls we've all known have always done when it starts cutting close to the bone. As I steered and stared and speeded, and listened to the insane, lovely rap of the Wolfman, I felt a high exhilaration overshadowing my tiredness; and I began to see the structure of the energies involved in our particular trip. I saw the energies, but it took years to understand them. I saw that it was Brooks and I who were pushing this show so hard. Red was restless and needed only a direction in which to move; we were moving and gave him that direction. Gardner wasn't going anywhere; one place was as good as another, so long as he didn't have to stay too long in any one of them. But he did want to spend a little more time somewhere, more time than we were prepared to spend. Renee had wanted the least expensive ride to Denver, and she'd got it. So it was me and Brooks.

For Don, it centered on money. He didn't have any and was borrowing from me whom he didn't know very well. He never did feel too secure without plenty of money. Don wanted to get back to Portland where he had a good job. (He wound up working days as a teamster, and nights as a bartender, such was Brooks' need and ability to work.) Until he had a job, money in his pocket and more coming in there was no way Don was going to let up, and at that time home was Portland. That's why he pushed, and I saw it then, going up the switch-backed, snow-filled turns of Berthoud Pass in a dawning 1959 blizzarding morning. What I couldn't understand so long ago but know well now is that fifteen years later Don would still be pushing, pushing on to the limits and sometimes farther, out there on the world's lost highways ahead of the Feds; pursuing the elusive dream that a job and Portland represented way back then. Who knows what represented it for my old friend and comrade while he was lost on the on the highways of the fugitive in America? While he was lost on those endless roads I thought of the words of the song: "May the longtime sun shine upon him/all love surround him/and the clear light within guide him home."

Eventually, it did.

I pushed for a different reason. For me it was a girl. There was a particular female person on the West Coast whom I wanted to see, and I wasn't going to let up until I was with her.

No matter that a few months later I could barely stand the girl, and her narrow mind, and empty head, and antiseptic spirit that I came to know only too well, and....ahhhhh....but that's another story, a long one. No matter, for if there's something on a man's mind he's not really going to rest until he understands it, has it, gets up it, falls off it, whips it, quits it, lets go of it or fucks it. No matter that only a few days before I was into ski racing and the girl didn't matter as much as the proper wax for the day. The races were over and it was the spring of a long season, and I wanted to see the girl bad enough to drive non-stop from coast to coast, missing everything along the way except that eternal concrete asphalt ribbon going nowhere and my fellow inmates of the great black gas-gobbling beast of the endless highway. I knew then, just at dawn, that I was pushing so hard for a girl and that knowledge made me want to push even harder; and I did, the great beast responding to the added surge of gas by fishtailing all over the road like the ass-end of a teeny-bopper in heat. From my present perspective I estimate, conservatively, that ninety-nine percent of the troubles, blues, hard times, desperation and general bullshit I have ever known have been related to women. I did not say 'created' by women, for each person, ultimately, creates the path of his own life and is responsible for it, and my hard times have not been created by the women I've known any more than Brooks' federal indictment was created by those pieces of paper and metal we call money. Though I had no tools to know that in 1959, since then I have seen Don and myself and the others push just as hard or harder for other things besides women and money; and so I know that it is an individual, personal matter, and that you pay dearly for pushing, pushing too hard, pushing the river, pushing that which is not yours to push; and I know that all members of the endless legions of the lost highway travelers will remain on the circular path of repetition until they ease up, learn the lesson, see the wheel of karma and get off it. And that's a hard one.

Just after daylight we passed Winter Park, and it had ceased to snow. The NCAA championships were being held at the time and we could see the downhill we all knew from other races. We had many friends in the races, and it would have been nice to have seen them and some of them would have appreciated our stopping but I was driving and no one made a definite suggestion that we stop, though Gardner wanted to I'm sure. So we pushed on through to Steamboat Springs, a town we all knew well, stopping for breakfast in our favorite restaurant.

We ate and drank coffee and read the Rocky Mountain News. The food and rest from the road and walking around gave us energy and we talked about our trip and the good day it was turning out to be and what we were doing and who we were, for then as always we worked hard to know, for sure, the answer to every man's question to himself—"Who am I?"

We hit the road again. I collapsed in the back seat and wasn't aware of another thing until early afternoon when I awoke in

Salt Lake City, my least favorite American city in those days. The Mormons, like all true believers riding on the words of others instead of the experience of self, turn me off. Also, less than a year later, I destroyed a leg and ankle in a downhill at Alta, spent several days in the local Catholic hospital recovering from an operation, and was told by Salt Lake's 'finest bone surgeon' that I couldn't ski for five years and would never race again. Unacceptable words for a twenty-one-year-old ski racer, and they were not accepted, though it was two years before the leg could be trusted. Nevertheless, now, after a few years of working at Alta summer camps, guiding and climbing in Little Cottonwood Canyon, making friends with some of the best locals, as well as some of the transients like myself and getting into the things I like while ignoring/avoiding those I don't, I've learned to regard Salt Lake City as one of the best places I know, as cities go. Strange, the changes.

We ate again and blasted into the homestretch—Salt Lake City to Reno, the fastest, most boring highway in the universe, across the indescribably lovely Utah/Nevada desert I have crossed hundreds of times and never seem to stop crossing. I made the trip again just a few weeks ago. Knowing we had a mere 580 miles to "home" gave us a jolt of juice we badly needed. On the last leg on our last legs. We had a flat tire in Wells, and night was on us before we got to Elko.

At around two in the morning we pulled up to the back entrance of my parents' tiny Reno apartment. We had been on the road for sixty-five hours. We unloaded about twenty pairs of skis from the rack and stored them in a corner of the living room. My fellow passengers immediately crashed on the floor in sleeping bags, but my fatigue wouldn't let me sleep. I showered, put on clean clothes and took a refreshing walk along the Truckee River. When I got back I joined my mates on the floor and I slept the sleep of colored dreams. In the morning I loaned Brooks enough money for a bus ride to Portland and saw him off. A week later he returned my money, paying me from his first check. Gardner hung around a couple of days, and when Reno made him nervous, he moved on down the line. Red stayed a bit longer and then just disappeared one day, driving off into the Northwest (I think) in his trusty black Oldsmobile. I got a job on a newspaper in Fallon, commuting 120 miles a day, and six days a week. Richard Nixon was going to try for the presidency in a year. It was a long summer.

THE NEXT STEP IN THE EVOLUTION of night-driving technique was the discovery of speed—the drug, not velocity—and discovery by the driver, not society at large, for people were using speed's unique violation of body and mind long before this driver ever wired himself through an endless night of headlights and steering wheel at the cost of several thousand Benzedrined brain cells. Speed comes in several forms, each playing its own, subtle, delicious variation on the central theme of the person using it. Unfortunately, all the individuals I know who have experimented enough to rate as connoisseurs are unable or unwilling to give a coherent description of the varieties of this drug's experience.

It is against the law to possess speed without a prescription, but like all things in public demand it can be easily obtained for the interested buyer. I have never used speed to get fucked up, though as a by-product of using it to get through a night or hard day I've gotten fucked up on it. It gets you past your fatigue, and will carry you across the country if you put enough of it into the right kind of system, but, as with all things, you pay for what you get. I've never understood those sonic souls who eat speed for kicks. That one is just too hard. But to each his own, so long as he gets through his own night to his own destination. Speed has taken me through many nights and a couple of days of driving, a few more days of school and work, and a party or two when I didn't want to slow down. I tried ski racing on it once, but I immediately realized my abuse.

They say that speed kills brain cells and 'they' are undoubtedly right, but then so do napalm, the M-16, the Smith-and-Wesson.38, the night stick and the lie, and 'they' never say anything about those abuses. It's my view that speed is a good friend of the night driver and like all good friends it is always helpful and will always be there and can never hurt you unless you abuse it. Then, of course, as with all things abused, you're on your own.

My remaining brain cells can't remember exactly when

speed came into the picture, but in 1961 I stayed up all night on a Greyhound bus between Salt Lake City and Reno cranked up on some speedy pill so I could read "On the Road" for the second or third time.

Everyone is different and reacts uniquely to each drug, but for me speed is not a social substance. The only time it's good for me is when I'm alone, more, when I'm driving alone through the night. The drug makes me too hyper to deal with myself, the task at hand (driving, for instance) and other people all at the same time. Marijuana and alcohol are social drugs, social suppositories even, but speed is for soloing.

One of the best experiences I've ever had with speed came in the fall of 1967. I was in Los Angeles, which has been called by reliable observers of the topic "the asshole of creation." I was in that most modern of cities for one of those yearly autumnal events, a ski show, part of that series of bizarre business/PR/fantasy/circus gatherings of people and industry and scams and scenes which bounce all over the U.S. of A. and which are so far removed from what skiing is.

At 9 p.m. on October 15, 1967 the hated ski show was over. The next day was my twenty-ninth birthday, and only were I bedridden with every bone broken, encased from head to toe in plaster like the great, white, bottle-fed mystery of Catch 22, crazed beyond mobility on elephant tranquilizers, or, of course, mesmerized by the love that will never die was I going to spend that night in the lost city of the angels. None of those ailments being my case at the time, I packed my bus, got a handful of yellow pills from Frankie Nemko, a friend and then-fellow-inmate of the Far West Ski Association office who had picked up the speedy little devils in an Ensenada drug store on a recent trip south of the border, blasted my way onto the nearest entrance ramp and locked on/tuned in/steeled down to the great freeway system of the sunshine state.

No sunshine there, if you know what I mean, but there were and are thousands of lights lighting the freeway and thousands of headlights lighting up the lighted concrete channels that bind together the centers of civilization in our mobile time and culture. Hard on the eyes as well as on the rest of the system, but with the help of Frankie and modern chemistry I was confident of getting through a night of flight from the angels that protect Los Angeles, fleeing in favor of the mountain spirits inhabiting the shores and waters and trees and rocks around beautiful Lake Tahoe (which already had begun to feel the crushing wheel rolling in every direction, pushed by the uncaring greed heads who developed South Shore into a circus-time San Jose and Incline into a third-class Monte Carlo, scarring the entire area with roads, 'real' estate developments and ugly, poorly-constructed buildings and billboards—and, let us not forget, also emptied undercover sewage into the south end of the Lake of the Sky, thus starting an irreversible spread of the self generating algae that clouds water and destroys life). Yes— yes, indeed!—it flashed through my trumpeting brain that

Tahoe was my country, the place where I grew up, and the one I knew best.

Yet in the last analysis and in the first feeling there is no difference in essence, in human motivation, between Los Angeles and Lake Tahoe and the concrete-freeway snake along which my VW slunk and the shabby housing tracts that rubbed out the fruit orchards of the once lovely Santa Clara Valley and a San Francisco Bay that man has shrunk in half and the rocks in Yosemite that would one day be painted over for a TV series called "Sierra" that foisted itself off on a gullible public with the ecologically in shuck of "a show about protecting nature from man." Isn't man part of nature? No difference at all. Yes. No. No difference. Raping the earth is rape, no matter whether it is Los Angeles or Lake Tahoe or Sun Valley or the north slope of Alaska and the leaky pipes moving south. And since even the slightest reflection on the unalterable, fragile chain of life and the beautiful/terrible march of evolution makes it obvious that earth is the mother-sustainer of all life here, including human life, the implications of plundering the earth are obvious. What kind of civilization, what kind of culture, what kind of people, are greedy enough, careless enough and—you know—stupid enough to violate their own mother, pollute her waters, poison the air she breathes, bury her alive under concrete/asphalt/brick/metal/plastic/glass piles of debris; and, in the name of profit, progress, patriotism, patrimony or pandemonium, destroy the clear channels and very systems by which she sustains her children and keeps the cycles going? I'll tell you what kind. My people have done this. And yours too. I don't mean my kind of people. I mean my ancestors; the progenitors of American culture, civilization and life values. The living meat of all who gave us life and sustains us is the very one that—in the same breath and movement and spurt of blood through the beating heart, in the sickness of that dark part of the human spirit that has always sold itself short—keeps trying with all its anti-life to sell us down the black, hopeless road to perdition. The human soul is the currency, and the devil the dealer. It has been the same since the beginning of creation, and all those walking dead Americans—those who have traded their own lives and the lives of their children and their children's children in on a Cadillac, a color TV and a material guarantee in life which there can never, in reality, ever be—have made a bad, stupid, indecent bargain that has put us all under a national/world debt that will not be an easy one to pay off, balance out and bring from the red into the black.

But it can be done and lots of us know it, only the debt can't be wiped out in a moment; nor can it happen without the concentrated effort, the centering of energy of a lot of people on planet Earth. Center where? Concentrate on what? Peace on earth? Happiness? Compassion? Love? Who cares? Just so long as it is done. Thy will be done. Find out who you are, and then do it. Climb a mountain. Build a home. Make a poem. Design a dome. Walk to Rome. Write a tome. Make your lady happy, man; make your man happy, lady. It don't matter none. Just turn on the light that's down there somewhere, and give it all the juice you got so everyone can see.

But there are a couple of ground rules—rules of the road, you might say. Take what you need, but take no more; if you can't talk about it, you probably shouldn't be doing it; you always pay for what you get, so make sure it's what you want; you can't buy happiness or peace of mind, but maybe you can sell them; go in peace; be gentle; ya get what ya give, so give good, brother, give good; be care-full; and be cool, or as that great African short story brings HOME so well to those ready to listen: "He who shits on the road will meet flies on his return."

Rolling down the Grapevine, sipping from a plastic cup of Thermos-bottle coffee, I washed down my second yellow pill, and thank you Miss Nemko and all the druggists of Mexico and the world for speeding me on my way through this night and all the other lonely nights of the wheel. The Grapevine. There are a thousand stories of horrible wrecks on the Grapevine, trucks losing their brakes at the top and, if they made it, coming to the bottom at 300 mph, their drivers turned into ancient, white-haired old men with skeleton hands fused to the steering wheel; eyes as big as saucers, deep as wells, with pupils the size of pinheads; gonads shrunk to the size of peas and retreated up behind the scrotum so far that only Julie Christie, Brigitte Bardot, the Virgin Mary, Tina Turner, Germaine Greer and the Mona Lisa, all combined into one, perfect, illuminated woman, in love with this whisper of the remains of the truck driver who aged 2000 years in three minutes of surviving the Grapevine could ever bring life, warmth, movement and the flowing river of love back into those desiccated progenitors of the future of the human race; ahhh, yes, the Grapevine's one of the many possible bitches in life, if you let it be that. But I don't, cruising amazingly slow in the old green bus considering the velocity of my nervous system, especially that biggest-of-all-nerves—the brain; shifting down, down, keeping cool, thinking how clever it was, after fifteen years of visiting Los Angeles via Highway 395, to figure out that, in a VW bus, it is faster to get to Kings Beach on the freeway through Sacramento than on the kinky east side of the Sierra Highway 395. Well, to make the long way faster took a lot of construction, concrete, money and covered-over land right up the middle of the Central Valley, that fertile bed of agriculture that feeds California and beyond and which has been opened up by all that material and energy; but as we were just beginning to learn (and learned very well over the years) that openness was not to include such hometown boys as Cesar Chavez and David Harris, which shows, as if it needed showing, that highways, skyways, byways and seaways don't really open things up very much at all. Do they? No. Not at all. The most valuable openings, explorations, discoveries and wealth will not be gained by putting a freeway through the Central Valley or a man on the moon, but instead, in the human mind, as unknown, unrealized and neglected by most homo sapiens as UFOs, yetis, the teachings of the wise and the forests and mountains and seas of this lovely planet that we have abused and fought over and plundered and roamed around and conquered and lost and forgotten and remembered so many times and through so many civilizations that, when it reached Nagasaki and Hiroshima, even the slowest among us could no longer claim innocence, non-involvement or unawareness that we must either change or perish. And even change is no guarantee. There are no guarantees. There is only life. Life and the universal laws that every person knows at each birth and every death, and a few obey in between.

For some reason I began thinking about my friend Fred Fogo. Fred and I had shared an office the year before while teaching English at the University of Nevada. Fred really appreciated the English language, and he'd memorized volumes of poetry. He had grown up in Gary, Indiana, and appreciating and teaching English was his ticket out of Steeltown, U.S.A. At one point during that year, he discovered the Haight-Ashbury, just a few hours west and not yet into the degeneracy that was to come. Old Fogo wasn't about to miss out on the Haight, and I wound up teaching his classes for a couple of weeks until he came around, which he did, naturally, like any good man rounding third base. What I remembered so clearly about Fred that night, as I blazed through the early-morning hours of California's Central Valley, was the time he gave a bit of Dylan to his class:

Then take me disappearin' through the smoke rings of
my mind
Down the foggy ruins of time, far past the frozen leaves
The haunted, frightened trees, out to the windy beach
Far from the twisted reach of crazy sorrow
Yes, to dance beneath the diamond sky with one hand
waving free
Silhouetted by the sea, circled by the circus sands
With all memory and fate driven deep beneath the waves
Let me forget about today until tomorrow

Then he asked them to punctuate it. Well, his class wasn't ready for that in 1967 Nevada.

I liked it so much I picked up on it and gave the same thing to my classes with identical instructions, except I also asked them to write a theme about whatever the words inspired in them. My classes weren't ready, either.

The only bigger depressions of my English-teaching career were the times I asked my students to write themes on their feelings, thoughts and ideas about capital punishment and Viet Nam. The murderous little bastards made Bill Calley seem like a misunderstood saint who'd had a little bad luck along the shining road to illumination. Less than a year later I was speeding through a dark night that marked another passing of the seasons, as easily observable on the freeways as in the forest, instead of grinding through a long night of grading papers written in a required course in English by people attending a

University, but distraught at an assignment to read one book—any book!! Mickey Spillane, Luke Short, Dostoyevsky, DeSade, Hemingway, Hesse or Irving Wallace; it didn't matter, just so long as they read something and write a report on it, to express through the English language whatever the book inspired in them. For the most part the response was grim—about what, in my naiveté, I would expect of sixth graders in a school for backward mongoloids. It was a strange, gruesome year in the English Department. The bright spots among the teachers were Fred and Ace. Fred, I think, finally got his Ph.D. and is out there someplace in the university system, short-circuiting it with jolts of Dylan and Fogo humor, which is very good.

Ace was on his way to Ph.D.-dom, and—as the best graduate student in the department, as well as the best poet—to a secure niche somewhere as a profession heavy until he ran into Gurdjieff, who turned him around and got him looking into the mirrors that the people around us provide for us to see ourselves and how we're doing. Who needs a Ph.D. when there are magic mirrors to play with?

Strange to be thinking of Fogo and Ace and the English Department as I approached Sacramento and washed another yellow devil down with black coffee while my eyes ached to close and rest. And I knew that even were I to gouge them out of their sockets those eyes would go on seeing, like distant satellites relaying information to my supersonic brain, lurching through the movements and momentum of keeping the show on the road until Kings Beach where there waited rest and a woman who, while not the possessor of a love that couldn't die or an uncooling kiss, never lied unless you got close enough to her to bring out her fear of discovering who she really was. Sad case. She later relinquished her mind to one of the Jesus groups promising the true/one/only/eternal/blessed path to wherever it is that such people crave to go, away from the present where, apparently, they are not really at. And even in the Sacramento morning of my twenty-ninth birthday, heading, at long last, east toward Auburn, the seeds of all that was to happen were planted and growing and obvious upon a little imaginative reflection. From L.A. to Kings Beach. Hmmmmmmmmm.

My body and brain were humming like those high-tension wires passed under in the hills above Santa Cruz on springtime runs, my eyelids twitched like shell-shocked soldiers re-entering society after 10,000 years on the front lines, and my hands perspired and shook on the wheel in time to a silent, secret, speed-freak's symphony of the road. The last leg of any journey is easier because the sighted end makes the juices flow, even the tired ones; but it's also the hardest time because there isn't much current left to mix with the juice; and me and the chemicals racing through my body were tuned into the homestretch; up out of the valley and into the gradual foothills of the Sierra and Highway 49, intersecting the main road between San Francisco and New York as it threads down from the north, through places with such unbeatable names as Sierra City, Downieville,

Nevada City and Grass Valley, and snakes up from the south, beginning in Oakhurst and continuing on into Mt. Bullion, Big Oak Flat, Moccasin, Angels Camp (made famous in this century by jumping frogs, shitting dogs and BearValley), Sutter Creek, Plymouth, Nashville, El Dorado, Placerville and, finally, Coloma, where it all started in 1848. One wonders why the road isn't called Highway 48, and all those gold-lusted crazies of yesteryear didn't go down in history as the 48ers. (And what if gold had been discovered twenty years later?) Whatever, Coloma can't be called the beginning of the rape of California; but it must be known as a pivot point in the continuing, violent destruction of the land that borders the Ocean of Peace. As if to remind me of the ever-present force and fact of karma, an almost perfect photographic image of something I read somewhere, sometime, flashed into my mind, like lightning from the ether, riveting me to myself with the knowledge of the connections between all people and places and times and oceans and streams and flowing rivers of thought and feeling and action:

> SUTTER, JOHN AUGUSTUS *(1803-1880), pioneer settler in California on whose land gold was discovered in 1848. He was born February 15, 1803, in Kandern, in the Grand Duchy of Baden, of Swiss parentage. He went to America in 1834, fleeing from bankruptcy and abandoning his wife and children. After traveling widely and experiencing further financial failures he reached*

California in 1839. By sheer charm and vivacity, supplemented by a claim to military rank that never existed, he persuaded the Mexican governor to grant him lands on the Sacramento River, where he was to establish a fortified settlement. There, at its junction with the American River, he established New Helvetia, later to become the city of Sacramento. He built Sutter's Fort, set up frontier industries, cultivated the land, and increased his herds. His debts were enormous and his tenure precarious, but when trappers and immigrants came to his fort they were received with lavish hospitality

At the outbreak of the war with Mexico (1846) the fort was taken over by U.S. forces commanded by John C. Fremont, who was unappreciative of Sutter's former kindness to American settlers. Sutter, nevertheless, gave invaluable aid to the conquerors and became an American citizen. Then, just as his fortunes seemed restored, the discovery of gold on his land ironically brought colossal disaster. On January 24, 1848, James W. Marshall, who was building a sawmill for Sutter at Coloma, 50 miles up the American River, arrived at Sutter's Fort and with great secrecy showed Sutter flakes of gold. The two men tried to keep the discovery secret but the news leaked out, and shortly there was wholesale desertion from New Helvetia, followed by swarms of gold seekers from San Francisco. Sutter saw his lands overrun, his herds slaughtered, and his property stolen. His downfall was completed when the courts denied title to his Mexican land grant. By 1852 he was bankrupt. There followed brief periods of hopefulness and illusory grandeur, but the rest of his life was one of continued disappointment and frustration. The family he had abandoned in Switzerland joined him after 16 years, only to share in his misfortune.

Sutter died in Washington, D.C., on June 18, 1880, heartbroken at the failure of Congress to act for his relief. Sutter Street, in San Francisco, and Sutter County commemorate his name; in Sacramento there is a restoration of his fort.

RISING OUT OF THE COUNTRY OF SUTTER'S GHOST and up into the Sierra, the last range of high mountains before the west end of the continent drops into the Pacific. And good mountains they are. It is nearly dawning upon a grey day, and my rocketing brain and numb body know that together they could go on and on, perhaps past the point of no return, like all those lost tribes of California Indians who were pushed and chased along the fugitive highways of their own nineteenth-century time, past the point of return, self-regeneracy and survival.

We know we will push as hard as we can get away with; but not that hard, not so the waters of life are undrinkable, the breath of life dangerous to breathe and the flesh of life infested with synthetics so cleverly constructed that hundreds of years will not return them to nature's cycles. No. That's too hard, and we must be as careful of being pushed as we are of pushing ourselves too hard. But I drive those freeways more than most, I think; my friends all enjoy the best that technology and the American dream have to offer; my taxes support the unspeakable aggression my country was committing in Southeast Asia and, a few years later, would repeat in a slightly different manner in Chile, my favorite country outside my own; and as I peered into the dawn of my twenty-ninth year, there was no way to avoid my own participation, involvement and entrapment within the very system that will destroy all of us, like Jews in the Dachau ovens, unless we take care of that system first.

After all, that system perpetuates only itself, making people dependent upon it, producing millions who would starve in a month if suddenly brought face-to-face with survival on planet Earth without the system; and people like me, approaching thirty, better-educated (according to the system) than most, but the possessor, through that education, of such basic survival skills as turning a set of skis both to the left and to the right; distinguishing nouns from adjectives—or which drugs will help you get where you want to go; using a shovel; doing the good-time basic stomp dance—or hundreds of calisthenics; reading thousands of books; typing; listening to music; knowing the geography, museums, bars, restaurants, resorts, highways and mountains of North and South America and Europe;

and driving through the longest, darkest, loneliest nights of the lost soul on planet Earth.

And just because we cannot escape the system and are, therefore, part of the establishment does not mean that we have to be part of, for instance, Richard Nixon's establishment, or Ronald Reagan's, or Nelson Rockefeller's or anyone else's. Since there is, in reality, no dropping out of the system, the one who thinks he has dropped out has really copped out and left the rest of us with the staggering chore of sabotaging, short-circuiting, sand-bagging, shaping up, turning on, fighting, changing, chopping, hacking, writing about or using whatever tools and talents we have to bring life into the machine, humanity to the robot.

As I crest the Sierra at the top of Donner summit and start down the east side I find myself looking at the flat, dull morning surface of Donner Lake, named after that group of unfortunate pioneers who, ultimately, fell into one of two categories: survivors, those who broke the taboo on cannibalism by eating the flesh of their friends and family who had died, in order to get through the longest winter night their souls will ever know; and non-survivors, who starved to death because they could not break down the barriers in their own minds concerning life's true priorities. And I never see Donner Lake without thinking of the good Dick Buek, that fine ski racer who died there and who, because he had courage, style, a flair for living and a true zest for life, was called "mad" by a less imaginative society.

It is light. I laugh and pour my last cup of coffee and start sipping it, guiding the green bus as if I were a part of its actual construction; and I laugh some more because I know that I really like turning skis left and right, playing with nouns and adjectives and even verbs, taking drugs, keeping my body in shape, reading, dancing, music, bars, restaurants, geography, museums and anything to do with traveling and mountains. Later, I learned about climbing; and that helped a lot.

The best thing I can do about anything is to take care of myself—polish the skills I enjoy, drop the ones I don't and keep myself open and learning and in the flow at all times.

Truckee is still asleep and strangely inactive, almost like an abandoned town, softly lit in the cloudy morning light of this new day that will probably turn into a rainy one. I think of friends and other times in Truckee as I head up the Truckee shortcut to Kings Beach. My body and brain and eyes are wonderfully tired, and I wonder if I am more tired because of the little yellow speed pills from Mexico than I would have been without them, and would I have made it this far without their added jolt to the personal system? The thought roared into my mind that we ought to be able to do with will and knowledge and preparation the same things we can do with any chemicals. If we were born perfect, if man was created in God's own image, then aren't the synthetic chemicals we put into our bodies to hide, help, slow down, speed up, change, fuck up or reveal to ourselves the essential nature only the unmistakable proof of our imperfection, our fall, and an indication of how far we really have to go along the road? My poor brain feels like a conscious, feeling Ferrari approaching a 120-mph turn at 130, but somehow assured—by some mysterious power higher than the laws of speed and turns and machinery, deeper than the instinctual knowledge of imminent danger—that everything is going to be all right and that you really can push it further and by doing it just right a 130-mph turn can be created out of the old 120-mph one.

Strange thoughts tumble through my brain. But, what the hell, it's my birthday and I've escaped Los Angeles for the time and I'm at my beautiful little cabin in the hills above Kings Beach. As I turn off the ignition and the engine quits and I look at the cabin and listen to the wind in the pines and hear the silence behind the wind and feel the quietness of the autumn mountains that surround Lake Tahoe, I am keenly aware of the spirit, infinitely more powerful than any drug or chemical that man may ever use to remind himself of his own spirit and the spirits that inhabit the land. As I get out of the bus I smile to be where I am, having used well the last nine hours. What the hell. It's my birthday. Might as well go inside and wake up the woman and celebrate having made it through another year and another night of the road and toast the knowledge that if the spirit is right and if the will is strong and if the drugs hold out, there are many years and many miles yet to go.

So far I've discovered only one other substance to put into the system that's really helpful for night driving. That is the root of the ginseng plant. I tried lots of others and, while usually interesting, I never found any I would recommend or use as aids through a night on the road.

Cannabis sativa, for instance, is one of the fine gifts mother earth gives her children, and it is really useful and pleasant in many situations. But driving through the night on weed is not my cup of tea. It would make a classic run—say, Sun Valley to Aspen—370,000 miles and 1000 years long, and that might be fine for someone who really enjoys driving, but I don't.

There have been some long hauls attempted, accomplished and aborted with the help of several of the standard hallucinogenics. They're all good friends and teachers, but to waste their energies and lessons on all-night driving is a little like trying to study advanced nuclear physics and its relation to the human soul in Tibetan while guiding a runaway truck down the Grapevine at 300 mph for fifteen hours. No sense watering good wine and driving the world's freeways is not even very good water.

There were, however, a couple of memorable rides that way. Once, after my first day of Sun Valley skiing in several years, and a good day at that, I ingested some of Owsley's best and cruised into the night toward Reno with two friends. I'm not, at the moment, into attempting to describe in detail that kind of trip, but we avoided certain death on the hood ornament of one of those huge semis that create typhoons of air waves when you pass them in the night time Nevada desert by changing drivers at just the right time. I heard for the first time on that trip the words 'Chouinard' and 'carabiner,' both of which were to become interwoven with my life within a couple of years.

When we arrived in Reno, just before a February dawn, tired and wired and ready to come down in the bed I had been away from for a week, my house was locked, something it had never been before. It took some time to roust my secured housemate and get inside to rest, but the signs were unmistakable and, in a few hours, I went to see the head of the University of Nevada English Department and told him there was no way I would ever again endure another deathly dull graduate seminar, a morbid sentence inflicted on people so lazy and unimaginative as to have nothing better to do than attend graduate school, a punishment specializing in creating a previously unknown and unnecessary 'problem' (trace the development of R.W. Emerson's writing, as seen in the history of American literature, beginning with Jonathan Edwards) and then talking that problem into the ground, nay, clear through the crust into the bowels of the earth and on out the other side, China, where the people are more intelligible than those experts on the English language who haunt graduate seminars. I retired from that world a few hours after that trip, and I never felt better, as if the fatigue of 10,000 years on the front lines had suddenly been removed.

Another time, Christmas Eve it was, I skied all day at Bear Valley, cleaned up the condominium a friend had loaned me, cleaned some magic cactus and hit the slippery road to Reno in my 1938 Chevy truck with the camper on the back. It had been a difficult, mind-crushing several weeks, and I was opened up and not healing quickly. So, as I chugged down the hill from Bear to the shortcut to Highway 88 over the Sierra, I sought the powers of teaching and healing found in the bitter medicine of the magic cactus. I bounced along in the beautiful old truck, plopped little dried pieces of cactus top in my mouth and forced myself through the unforgettable taste.

It was a solo trip, but as we have all learned, or need to learn, there ain't no soloing possible on spaceship earth. I was averaging, maybe, 35 mph through the cold, clear night. This suited me, as there was no hurry or reason to be anywhere but where I was. My tape deck was broken, so except once when I stopped for gas there was just me and truck and the power. Until, that is, I had been going for several hours without seeing another car, careening along a snow banked path that for all I really knew was nothing less than the maze of the eternal mandala that leads to the self we all seek; and then, almost as if I were hallucinating—and that was the first possibility I checked out— right near Silver Lake on Kit Carson Pass, the most desolate, isolated, coldest section of Christmas Eve Highway 88, there was this dude walking along with a dog, a backpack and a pair of red plastic snowshoes sticking out the top of his pack. I could hardly believe it. But, then, no one should spend Christmas Eve alone and I laughed as I stopped to pick him up.

His name was Tom, and he wanted to make sure it was okay for his dog to get in before he'd accept a ride. I laughed again and motioned the two of them inside. Tom was from the Bay Area, and he'd been snow camping for five days near Silver Lake, just him and his dog. He figured his mind was cleared out enough to return to the city, his family, his past, his future, his problems and all the other realities of his personal fate. He began talking about it almost immediately. I offered him some peyote. He said he wasn't into that kind of thing and complimented me on my safe driving. Tom gave it all to me—his whole story—as if I were father confessor, garbage can, bank, trusted friend, diary and repossesser from the mortgage company all in one. Tom was twenty-one years old and we talked over his whole life.

It was easy to see the beginning of the solution to his problem—he was blaming his family for not picking up what he wouldn't pick up himself. Who among us doesn't know that one? I told him what I thought and all I knew about such things which included the necessity of speaking up, discussing and letting out what you think and how you feel at the moment, which reminded me to tell Tom to get his fucking feet off the dashboard, as I have a personal code that a person will treat you the same way he treats your car, and if Tom and I were going to be friends he couldn't put his feet on my dash or on me.

That blew his mind. The connection had been made. We talked non-stop after that and by the time we passed Woodfords and left the Sierra for the Carson Valley, the teachings were coming home. By the time we entered Washoe Valley the healing had begun. Tom by this time had decided to try to make it home for Christmas. I dumped him and his dog and his snowshoes by the freeway to San Francisco, and he wasn't there a few hours later. I went to my father's house. He was still up watching late-night television behind the traditional hot toddy. He offered me one but I refused, telling him I had another thing going. He laughed and we talked and then my brother came home and we all talked and then it was time to sleep.

But of course the best way through or to anything is clean: that is, relying on your self; letting what's inside provide the fuel rather than counting on the handiwork of some druggist who, for all anyone knows, may be mixing his concoctions the morning after an all-nighter from Tijuana to San Francisco, wired out of his brain on some Mexican yellow devils put together by some loco early the morning after he had fired through the night from, say, Hermosillo to Ciudad de Mexico with his mind laying in his lap, full of the powders he bought from a brujo in the hills who, in turn, had walked without sleeping for three days through the mountainous desert, chewing a series of dried, horrible-tasting little things given him by a friend who had a teacher who lived on air and hadn't slept in forty years, and who, it was rumored, didn't need to go out of himself or put anything into himself in order to know everything he ever wished to know.

Which brings us to the advantages of such naturally growing substances as peyote, ginseng, cannabis sativa, chia seeds, etc.,etc.—the druggist is absolutely reliable.

Cosmic Carl turned me on to ginseng. I even remember the date I first used it—August 3, 1969—and August third has since become a date when strange things happen to me, one of those days that turns the course of life, a day that would ground me on the rocks if I let it. But I won't, though the day must be passed with caution. Back to the subject. Ginseng. The mind is like an unruly child who refuses to sit quietly in the corner, drawing with his crayons in a coloring book; instead, he yells, colors the walls with crayon and generally refuses to be the little angel he is told he must be. And, yes, ginseng.

Steve Wood and I made plans to climb the Steck route on Mt. Morrison, above Convict Lake, not far from Mammoth—the beautiful, spectacular face inescapably seen by every steamed-out drunk who ever returned from Hot Creek before dark. I had been there before, a few weeks earlier, with a different partner. But it wasn't his place and we'd had to abort. In the meantime Lito and Cado climbed it in two days. They said it was good. I wanted to do it badly and I wanted to do it in a day. I knew it would be a long day. I was living at Squaw at the time, so I went to see Cosmic Carl at the health food store in Tahoe City. I was looking for some Sportade which Carl had never heard of. I told Carl I needed something to help keep me going when very tired, and Cosmic Carl knew exactly the ticket. He said to try these little capsules of ginseng he was selling for twenty-five cents each. That seemed pretty expensive for a capsule, but I'd paid more for less. And anything that costs that much must be good. Right? I took ten.

I left Squaw the afternoon of the second and drove to Mammoth where Steve was working. We got organized and picked up Steve Thompson, who was hiking in to the base with us for the exercise and would carry out sleeping gear which we hoped we wouldn't need on the climb. Steve Thompson, the brother of racers Lance, Perry and Tim, was just re-learning to walk after nearly two years of casts, crutches and operations necessitated after he straddled the tree-size finish post of a downhill in Steamboat. We drove to Convict Lake late in the afternoon and began the four hour bushwhack to the base of Mt. Morrison. It was hot and every possible insect abounded. The hike was a drag. We ate dinner quickly and bedded at dark. There was very little sleep that night in the boulders at the base of Mt. Morrison. The heat was oppressive. The bugs were impossible. Apprehension was perceptible. I figure I slept two hours.

We were up before dawn and climbing in the first light after saying so long to Thompson, who wished us luck and hiked out. This day, which gave me one of my best mountain experiences, started out with a good sign. I found a better way to start the climb than the first time I'd been there, saving us almost two pitches of roping up. We moved fast, and didn't get lost once on a very complex route. We ran out of water before noon. By two in the afternoon we were both hurting from the hard-labor summer dries. It began to rain as Steve led up the great red chimney, and I was desperate enough to be grateful for the few raindrops I caught in my open mouth with my head thrown back. At about three o'clock we found water; we stopped, drank our fill, ate, took a ginseng and continued to the summit. We reached the top about 4:30. We signed and read the summit register, including a terse message from a member of the first party to climb the Steck route in winter: "never again." Then we began one of the longest, grungiest, most involved, difficult, shittiest descents in the Sierra. We reached Convict Lake about 9:30 that night and went straight to Mammoth. We showered and drank twenty glasses of orange juice from the cafeteria machine. Then I ate some more ginseng, watched Steve ease off to bed and hit the road to Squaw. About 2:30 in the morning I got to my tiny apartment under the tram, woke Jane and stayed up until dawn talking about the climb, Steve Wood, the descent, the orange juice at Mammoth, the drive, the mountains, the ginseng and what a wonderful life it was to be able to climb and to come home and talk until the summer Sierra dawn, with no thought of what the future might bring or the past may hold, enveloped in the unimaginably perfect present, talking with someone I loved.

I DIDN'T BECOME COMPLETELY AWARE of my disposition toward night driving until 1968, when we drove from California to Argentina. Though it should have been obvious years before, I didn't see it because it was such a natural part of the way I lived/live that, without giving it much thought, somewhere deep down in my mind, I assumed that everybody not only had his own nights of the road but the ability to get through them. That, I learned, is not necessarily the case.

Doug Tompkins, Yvon Chouinard, Lito Tejada-Flores and I started that six month trip from Yvon's shop in Ventura. In Lima, we added a fifth member, our English friend, Chris Jones. We had a 1965 Ford Econoline van; four surfboards; six pairs of skis; eight ropes; enough climbing equipment to get up anything under 25,000 feet; two 16mm movie cameras and more film than any one of us could carry at one time; a Nagra tape recorder with earphones; twenty-five hours of our favorite music on tape; our personal belongings, including clothes that would cover us from penetrating the tropics of Central America to skiing the volcanoes of southern Chile to climbing in Patagonia; camping gear, including mosquito netting to sleep in; wetsuits for winter surfing in Peru; books; and all the other outer and inner .necessities of our lives. It was a good trip, and we drove more than 18,000 miles before it was over.

As always happens when people are thrown, brought, dragged or fated and given enough time together, we soon became quite aware of the strengths, weaknesses, skills, inclinations, follies, shortcomings, characters, personalities and mentalities of ourselves and our mates within the situation at hand. Water seeks its own level. People, too. And without a word being spoken, or a conscious working-out of each man's part in the whole, I found myself the steady driver on the graveyard shift. I drove a lot of those 18,000 miles in the dark with all or most of the others asleep. Since we were passing through the borders of several of the most militaristic, suspicious, backward countries of the world, with jail and justice reputations bad enough to make us want badly not to get involved, we agreed beforehand to travel in a manner so as to make Mr. Clean seem, by comparison, the dirtiest, skunkiest, smelliest, most suspect traveling salesman ever to be caught crawling out of your thirteen-year-old daughter's bedroom window at dawn. And so we did, with me unbelievably accomplishing some of the longest, hardest night driving of my career, completely straight.

I had some astonishing (to me) adventures and lessons and experiences and, you know, revelations on the nighttime roads of South America during that trip. None of them was more memorable than one night in the Andes of Columbia, along the mountainous, Pan American dirt highway that twists through some of the weirdest, most uncomfortable country of the mind that I have ever passed through. We found ourselves on the nighttime Andean roads of Columbia almost by accident.

The Pan Americano ends at Panama for a few hundred miles; the engineers haven't yet figured out a way to put a highway through the swamps, bogs, jungles and other unknowns of the south of Panama. So, at the canal you either put your car on a boat or you turn around and head back north. We wanted to find a ship going down the Pacific side to Buena Ventura, or, even better, Guayaquil; but there wouldn't be any for two weeks, and in addition to our common, nervous inclination for the road Panama is one of the last places any of us would have chosen to spend two weeks. We found an alternative in a Spanish freighter which would take us and the Ford to Cartagena for a reasonable fee. We careened across the isthmus, from Panama City to Colon, caught our ship and spent two days in the Caribbean getting to Cartagena.

Cartagena—the heroic city, yesterday's queen of the sea is farther north than Panama. A sad, interesting place, full of memories and history and the vibes of the Spanish lust and greed that founded Cartagena, the same that made short work of the Inca and Aztec civilizations. We spent part of a day walking around, waiting for the car to be brought up from the bowels of the ship; as soon as the car was on the dock we got on the road, and we didn't want to stop until we reached a place called Playas, in Ecuador, where Chouinard, the surfing expert, informed us Mike Doyle had reported excellent surfing and sympathetic surfing people.

And so it came to be; but not without a more-than-fifty-hour grind, making only the minimum necessary human and mechanical pit stops of life on the road. There were two reasons for our haste: first, we wanted the Pacific surf; and, second, in those days the reputations of the bandits who lived in roving bands in the mountains of Columbia did not instill confidence in the peaceful, unarmed traveler. Indeed, a week after we passed through a bus on the same road was stopped by one of these bands, and more than twenty people were reported shot. Not too long before that drive, we had been surrounded by an army patrol in the hills near Antigua, Guatemala; the soldiers kept us covered with submachine guns and vibes that could turn blood to ice, especially those from one fellow who had the aim on Yvon and I—the first human being I had ever seen who I knew wanted badly, deeply and truly, to kill me.

"Did you see that dude's eyes?" Yvon asked me after they had left.

"Yup, sure did."

They'd kept us wondering if we had driven our last mile until we could convince them that we were only tourists, not "revolutionaries" (i.e. CIA) and, for sure, only passing through. Two weeks after this incident, the U.S. Ambassador to Guatemala was machine gunned to death in his limousine in downtown Guatemala City while on his way home for lunch. We had heard other stories, including the one about my old schoolmate, Bob 'Spade' Moran, who, as it turned out, was a CIA agent and died as a consequence; he met his end with two shotgun blasts in the back while walking down the main street of a tiny Guatemalan town, from two local fellows who did the job for a hundred dollars. So we knew that insanity was real, and we suspected a full measure of it existed in the mountains of Columbia. That was our feeling, anyway, and one measure of saneness is the ability to listen to the music of the gut twanging away on the central nervous system.

One of those nights I found myself behind the graveyard wheel of our journey, peering into the headlight-brightened dirt roads that wind through the strange, high jungle mountains of Columbia. Everyone was asleep—Yvon on the sleeping platform clear in back, Doug on the back seat and Lito sleeping shotgun on the other tiny front seat. I had the Nagra going, with the earphones on, plugged into the best music of the time. One side of a tape lasted nearly an hour, and every hour I would nudge Lito and have him change tapes. He would grunt and ask me how it was going, change the tape, offer to drive when I wanted and collapse back into one of the most uncomfortable positions in the history of sleep. So my company that night was Bob Dylan, Judy Collins, Leonard Cohen, Buffalo Springfield, Joan Baez, Tim Buckley, The Byrds, Quicksilver, the Jefferson Airplane and, of course, the Beatles, all good friends of the night, the day and all those grey times in between. Good music is one of the very best ways through long drives or, for that matter, any difficulties.

The most amazing thing happened that night. I didn't begin

to notice it until after five or six hours of driving, and my system was twanging and twitching in time to the music and the rhythms of the road, like a puppet being moved by the cosmic puppeteer in the universal control room.

The first things I noticed were the small bushes and trees alongside the road. I could see the potential animal spirit in their vegetable matter. Fair enough. I could understand and get my head into that one. Feed a carrot to a rabbit and the carrot becomes rabbit, not vice-versa; although, in the long haul, every rabbit is a potential carrot. The cycle of life, inextricably connected to the inescapable karmic wheel, turns over everything in its journey, making carrots out of rabbits, grass out of men, horses out of grass and glue out of horses with no more feeling or regard for the individual rabbit or blade of grass or man than the engine of the Econoline had for the individual molecule of the gasoline that propelled it along the Andean road, guided by a particular hunk of flesh and bones and blood to which I was presently attached and which would, inescapably, hopefully, help nourish a stout pine tree, a strong sagebrush or, at least, a blade of mountain-meadow grass.

Then I saw the tiny rodents trapped in the little shrubs along the road; the deer waiting to spring from the leafy trees on the hillsides lit up by the Ford; coyote-like creatures, crouched in expectant stillness among unnamable, formless ferns; half-dog, half-pig beasts, magnificently ugly, loping though the tall grass, stopped in mid-stride like the protected, unburnt silhouettes left on the streets of Hiroshima by terrified, running, doomed people; skeletal horses, staring dully into the lights from the structure of strange trees with roots so deep you could feel their permanence; flying frogs, stopped in mid-flight on the branch of an enormous, pine-like tree; powerful, lovely leopards and tigers, stopped in the act of the kill and the run of freedom and the pleasure of movement like the petrified mummies of Pompeii, embedded in the dirt-rock banks of the Pan-Americano highway; almost-human beings stretched out on trees in lifeless dejection, as if needing just one missing part— an eye, a heart, a brain, a toe, a kidney, a spleen or, perhaps, a soul—in order to start dancing to the sounds of The Grateful Dead, right there in the mountain jungles of Columbia; iguanas and snakes and spiders and bizarre birds everywhere, on every bush and tree, caught in the limb and the leaf, locked in the inanimate, waiting, waiting for the key, the time, the turn of the karmic, evolutionary, magic wheel of life and mystery that will plug them into the universal river of love and give them freedom, movement, substance—meaning. A whole menagerie of the mind accompanied me and my musical friends through that night.

Along toward dawn, that time of the morning when you can't see any difference in the night, but you feel the light will soon appear in the east, after, maybe, seven or eight hours behind the wheel, the entire show began to move. The zoo came to life on me. Deer; rabbits; coyotes; creatures not yet created, and others long gone; snakes; bears; lizards; an entire Fillmore ballroom rocking out to the Airplane, men and women dancing with crocodiles and water buffalo and pythons; flying frogs and hopping toads, four feet long; alligators; pigeons; eagles; bats; dogs; guanacos; cats of every description and size; every critter that ever existed in the human mind had stretched its vegetable limbs, broken the fibrous bonds that tied it to the earth and was on the move, all over the road and the banks and in the trees and flying through the sky.

Needless to say, I was fascinated. I don't know how long I moved through this swirling, primordial world, the gas-eating beast in my hands just another innocent creature of the jungle, the road and the mind, before I noticed an enormous mastodon standing in the road ahead. A 100,000-foot precipice was on the left, a sheer bank rose up on the right, and we were moving too fast to stop. I quickly considered the alternatives, slammed on the brakes, shifted down, braced myself for the inevitable crash with a mastodon and skidded right through the fucker to a stop.

Lito, by this time, had emerged from his back-breaking sleep and was peering around like a suspicious gnome waking up from a twenty-year long nap to a sound he couldn't quite recognize.

"What's happening, man?"

"I think you'd better drive," I said.

"Sure, sure, right on," he said, coming immediately to life.

I opened the door and stretched and my body was numbness in the flesh. I noticed that it was daylight and I was surprised. We were somewhere in the mountains and the morning cool refreshed me. My mind was working only on the most basic level. The road was dirt. The trees and bushes and flowers and ferns and shrubs and grass were vegetable. We were men and Yvon, a really good one, woke up and gave me the back sleeping platform, which I badly needed.

Lito, one of the worst drivers in the history of the wheel, took over. Lito has a faculty for learning that is unequaled by most human beings, but he drove the great Ford for six months during that trip without learning how to shift into second without grinding the gears. I suspect he never learned to drive so he wouldn't have to.

I crawled in back and covered myself with a down bag, oozed the remainder of my head into a sweater used as pillow and savored the delicious relaxation that massaged the tension from my body. I was already missing that wonderful, innocent world that began when I saw the animal spirit trapped in vegetable matter, and ended when we drove through that damned mastodon into another day. And why do we think we miss anything? Do we feel the loss of reality? Of illusion? Opportunity lost? Or is it only the realization of having encountered one more of God's thousand faces, all of which we must learn to know intimately, one by one, before we will be able to see the whole. I was awake when we started moving, but already dreaming in technicolor by the time Lito gnashed his way into second gear.

Another night on that trip, driver's fatigue helped set up a situation that taught me much, though like many lessons of the road and elsewhere I didn't see it right away. We didn't even drive all night, but after dinner at an amazing roadside restaurant in the desert of northern Chile it was my turn at the wheel. Our goal was Antofagasta by morning because the car was barely running, and we hoped to find parts there. No such luck, as it turned out. Eventually, we had to limp clear into Santiago at 20 mph where Yvon and Doug rebuilt the engine.

I don't remember much about the drive, but sometime about two in the morning we reached a gravel pit off the road just outside Antofagasta. I pulled in, turned the lights and engine off and, according to my habit, pulled on the emergency brake and put the beast in reverse gear. Then the five of us stumbled through the tired motions of getting ready to sleep. Chris and I slept on the ground behind the van, Yvon crashed just in front, Doug curled up on the sleeping platform and Lito had the back seat.

Sometime later, after all of us had quit the bed-down chit-chats and were sleeping deeply, Doug awoke to the instant realization that the car was moving. Doug is that kind of person, for the car couldn't have moved more than a foot. Since he was completely encased in his mummy bag, he flung himself headfirst, like a huge jumping worm, across Lito and the motor casing between the two front seats. He hit the brake with his hands. Lito woke up screeching and Doug was yelling for Yvon to get out of the way, and Yvon woke up with the front wheel stopped about six inches from his head. Chris and I woke up about the same time to the commotion.

Well, I took a lot of shit then and during the next few days for not putting the car in gear or using the emergency brake. Doug was most vehement in his shit-giving. It didn't help that he hadn't gotten over an unfortunate meeting with a Peruvian mule several nights earlier when it was late, we were a few hundred miles north of Lima and, once again, I was at the wheel while the others slept. I had been plugged into the Nagra and my musical friends, sighting down one of the skinniest paved roads on earth. Every time a truck came along, heading in the other direction, it was like trying to run a very tight, closed gate at 60 mph. The periodic adrenalin rushes caused by every passing truck helped keep me awake and provided a counterpoint to the music filling my head from the earphones. The beast was cruising at a steady 60 mph, our agreed-upon max. Suddenly, with no more warning than a few feet of headlight vision, we were surrounded by mules. Mules everywhere and they just kept appearing, all over the road. There must have been a thousand of the dumb creatures.

"Shit," I shouted.

Lito, riding shotgun, woke up mumbling, "Oh fuck, oh fuck, oh shit."

I steered the metal monster through a maze of mules like a broken-field runner on a speeded-up film. At one point an old Peruvian mule-tender complete with staff, flashed through my vision. We were getting to the other end, the van careening all over the place, everyone awake now, anything not tied down bouncing all over the inside like keno balls in the blower, clear highway in sight, when I clipped one of the mules in the ass with the right front bumper. The beast went down like he'd just been hit by a ton of steel moving at 60 mph, and the right headlight went out. The vehicle shuddered. I saw the mule thrashing around in the rear-view mirror. We cleared the herd and were still moving and on the road. I stepped up the pace to 70 mph and got the hell out of there.

"Genius driving, Dorworth, genius," Lito said.

And he was right. By all rights, we should have destroyed thirty mules and one Ford and all its inhabitants; but we'd got by with one mule with unknown injuries, a crunched fender and a broken headlight. The car was fixed in Lima for a few dollars. Doug, who didn't appreciate his luck at being alive after surviving the mule herd, apparently felt I should have flown the Ford over the beasts on the road, and landed on the other side.

My protests of innocence from negligence in both these cases were in vain. No matter what I said, thought, knew or claimed as habit, the car did start moving in the gravel pit and would have hit Chouinard if Doug had been one foot slower.

I didn't want to think I was that sloppy, and I didn't think I'd neglected those basics of the stopped automobile, but sometime after we'd gone to sleep the car had started rolling.

After the incident in the gravel pit, everyone got rearranged, the car was put in gear and the emergency brake pulled on; Yvon moved uphill from the great metal creature; and we all dropped into the deep and special sleep of the long-distance traveler, those questioning, but hopefully, not questionable souls who need to travel long distances. The next morning I was exhausted. Sometime after daylight, but well before any of us were ready to move, a force, a power, a voice that spoke not in words—something—wanted me to roll over and look at the sky. Nothing doing. I was secure and asleep and comfortable, and I didn't want to look at anything except the back of my eyelids and the whole of my dream. More persistent. "Roll over, you blockhead," it seemed to say. "No. Nothing doing. It's nice where I am. Why should I move?" I even stiffened my body against--what? I don't know. Just against. But after a time of arguing with a power that was going to have its way, no matter what, I rolled over and opened my eyes.

And there was a buttermilk sky scudding by above me, moving inland from the early September Pacific. I stared at the soft, friendly whiteness, and I sensed in a flash that the sky and I were one, that I was the universe and the universe was me; the whole of creation was within and I was the whole; and any differences I perceived between, say, myself and a buttermilk sky, or between anything else—a Martian and a human, an Indian and a White Man, a long and a short hair, a panda and a rock—was a result of the workings of a mind crazed on illusion. A mind addicted to drawing distinctions, separating, comparing, splitting hairs and atoms. A mind, as described by Walter Van Tilberg Clark, as wanting to be all instead of wanting all to be; a mind that attempts to limit the limitless. I saw that, in reality, everything in creation is connected, a part of the same whole, the same creation, woven together from fibers made of the same substance which, at bottom, is pure spirit, the divine spirit that breathes life and movement and rhythm into the universe.

When that realization had sunk into my brain and being, I rolled back over and fell immediately into a calm sleep.

A long time later the seeds planted that morning grew into a beautiful, sturdy, fruit-bearing tree. And eating the fruit of that tree teaches one to beware of habit. Habit is the great deceiver. Habit is the child of the machine, trying to make an experience, a time, a thought or action the same as any other. No matter how good, worthwhile or beneficial in the beginning, habit always ends up draining the life out of action, the juice out of thought and meaning out of result. Habit is a stagnant pool, making one moment like another; it is, therefore, corrupt and pestilential. Life is a clear, flowing stream; and each day, each minute, each instant must be met on its own terms, fresh, forever changing and irretrievable. Habit becomes system; system becomes machine; machine is death. The life force adapts to the situation at hand according to the intelligence of the moment, not the acquired habit of other times. Habit is faithless and will abandon and deceive: it will tell the brain that it has put the car in gear and pulled on the emergency brake, but it will forget to tell the body the same. Habit, which is not the same as practice, is a deceiver in the guise of friend; but habit never teaches the lay of the land and, sooner or later, leads its poor, trusting follower right into the quicksand of the mind that separates, splits, draws imaginary lines of division upon the indivisible and looks for differences instead of sameness, in much the same spirit as the man worrying about the splinter in his brother's eye, entirely ignoring the plank in his own. Life has to be embraced, with no holds barred, throwing the whole show on the line as if there were no tomorrow and no yesterday either!

WELL, THERE HAVE BEEN A LOT OF DRIVES in South America, North America and Europe, and there will be others in unknown places as well as along the well-worn routes. There have been nights I don't even remember, others I could reconstruct minute-by-minute. There have been drives with lady friends that were interrupted at some god-awful hour when one of us started messing around—leading, inevitably, thankfully, grace-fully to a mad searching for the first place to turn off and get into a delightful romp around the steering wheel or a more-down-to-earth roll in the sand and sagebrush before continuing with the perpetual journey, somehow refreshed, relaxed and realigned.

There was the time Brooks and I left Jackson at dusk in his Porsche and pulled into Reno less than ten hours later, without having spoken twenty words between us. I remember driving alone, non-stop, from Dallas, Texas, to Provo, Utah, in twenty hours and then being unable to sleep until I had showered and eaten. And Tony Racloz and I once drove from Los Angeles to Dallas, on our way to New Orleans to catch a freighter to Chile, in a drive-away car with thirteen pairs of skis sticking out the right rear window; we napped a few hours in the desert near Twenty-nine Palms, and again in a more vast desert near El Paso, but it was a grinding trip. Andi Schaal and I once pushed under deadline pressure from Whistler Mountain, British Columbia, to San Francisco, driving through the night in the old green bus equipped with a bed which we both used.

Once there was also a most amazing journey from Heidelberg, Germany to Fontainebleau, France and back with a German of killer blood, who had joined the French Foreign Legion when his own army became unemployed after WW II, and a Hungarian refugee from the 1956 fiasco. We drove a huge Mercedes truck and conversed in Italian, me and the Hungarian, who translated into German for the killer, who couldn't order a sandwich in French after five years in the French Foreign Legion and who hated every people except the Germans. And there have been night treks from places like Elko, Nevada, to

Yosemite; Seattle to Sun Valley; Val Gardena to Heidelberg; Bariloche to Buenos Aires; Salt Lake to Ketchum; Los Angeles to Nogales; Aspen to Reno; Ukiah to Reno; Lovers Leap to Gilroy; Los Angeles to San Francisco; and Boyne Mountain, Michigan, to Collingswood, Ontario. There have been a lot of nights on the road.

The last really hard solo, Jackson to Reno, summed up the entire situation for me. Opened my head a few degrees, yes, indeed, and created or, at least, recognized and fertilized the seed that is still growing into this piece of writing.

It was late July of a strange summer, and it was time to head to Los Angeles, via Reno and San Francisco, to catch a plane to wintertime Argentina. Time to put the skis back on and earn enough money to get through the fall. The VW bug was sporting a new motor, which was comforting, but it made 45 mph the mandatory limit for a while. It was, on the surface, just a six week trip down south—no big deal. But the vibes were wrong.

I headed out of Jackson late one July afternoon filled with the weirdest feelings, caused by crystal-clear signs from the hearth of the wanderer, unreadable at the time but naturally written in florescent letters a foot high in the vision of hindsight. I picked up a hitchhiker at the Teton Village road and headed over Teton Pass at 30 mph. My rider was a nineteen-year-old boy who had just hitched his first trip around the western U.S. He was heading for Seattle, and I could take him to Twin Falls. His name was Jim—a curious soul, full of questions and possible

directions—and we talked nonstop for the seven hours it takes
to drive to Twin Falls from Jackson in a VW with a new engine.
We talked about the education of the traveler; the dangers of
traveling; the highs and lows of the hitchhiker; the coffee I was
drinking and the ginseng I was eating; Richard Nixon (he quit
two weeks later); Argentina; skiing; an old DU ski racer, Ron
Downing, whom Jim worked with; Stephen and the farm in
Tennessee; farming; climbing; school; flying saucers; abortion;
unemployed Lockheed Ph.D. engineers in Seattle; girlfriends;
children; Buddha and the eight-fold path; Ken Kesey; and
toward Twin Falls, destiny, fate, free will and the crossroads. A
little after ten o'clock that night I dropped him on the freeway
to Boise and points north, and I went my own direction.

I left the Magic Valley farming country that borders the
Snake River and headed into southern Idaho and eastern
Nevada, along a route I have traveled so many times that I know
it the way most people know their backyards. I also know it is
more than habit that has had me repeating the same path for
more then twenty years with no end in sight, and I pay particularly close attention to the lessons and thoughts and feelings
and experiences of the highway in the east of Nevada.

Across the Snake River, where that patriotic, redneck hick-
turned-streetcrazy/motorcycle-stuntman/showman/pro-
moter/bullshit-artist, Evel Knievel, would soon reveal to the
world—like those doomsday evangelists who keep having to
change the prophetic date of the apocalypse as the day passes

by—the true colors of the con man, and they ain't red, white and blue. Strange to be quoting Suzy Chaffee; and I remember the time I gave a showing of the Fitzroy film in Sun Valley for the benefit of my old friend, Willy Bogner, who knows a lot about film-making. I was sure Willy would like and be surprised by this unusual film, and I was very anxious to get his reactions. Among others, the great skier, Hermann Goellner, and the great women's liberationist, Suzy Chaffee, attended. The movie has a section about the fifteen consecutive days Lito, Doug, Yvon, Chris and I were trapped by the weather in an ice cave on Fitzroy. The film is also about climbing the mountain. When the film was over, Suzy stole the show.

"How did you ever survive fifteen days up there without us women?" she asked.

Well, it was an unanswerable, especially since we did survive. But it must be admitted that Susie did get right down to the eeny-weenie of Evel's great Snake River nose dive when she said, "Definitely a case of premature ejaculation of the drogue chute."

No way to know all that in July, but, like everyone else, I wondered what Evel was really up to, and how he would pull it off, as I crossed for the uncountable time the bridge outside Twin Falls that has always signified to me, more than anything else, closeness to Sun Valley.

On through Twin Falls where Lerude and I ripped off tires more than twenty years earlier, and out into the desert toward

Jackpot. By then I had rigged up the Panasonic, battery-run cassette machine; and, since it looked to be a long night, got myself ready for some musical company. I chose The Eagles, good friends and musicians, for a starter, never suspecting that I would get so caught up in the album that I wouldn't change it or shut it off until I merged with Reno, eleven hours later.

> *Well, I'm runnin' down the road*
> *tryin' to loosen my load*
> *I've got seven women*
> *on my mind,*
> *Four that wanna own me,*
> *Two that wanna stone me,*
> *One says she's a friend of mine.*

That's it. Owners, stoners and friends. The first six are a dime a dozen, a nickel a six, less than a penny apiece; but the seventh—the seventh!—well, that is precious. The ones who want to own you surround every hype that ever came down the line; those who want to stone you are lingering around the outside of every turn on the road, the harder the turn the more of them there are, as if some natural law were in operation; but the friend, the one who is there where she says she is, the one who won't deceive, betray or belittle, the one you can grow with, talk with, laugh with, trust with, make it around the hard turns with, hope with and live with—well, that's a little more difficult.

Oh yes, indeed, "she's a friend of mine" is felt and known to be in the universe; but she isn't in the VW with the unbroken-in engine; and she isn't on the highways of the world, for the lost roads are teachers and paths but not friends, and she isn't anyplace you've ever been, old bearded traveler, though you've been close, and one of those endless roads leads there and....

Take it easy

Take it easy

The wheels whir through the night and the ginseng root under my tongue keeps a bearable taste in my mouth. Ginseng and black coffee. I try to remember nights I have invested in the road to the one woman—"she's a friend of mine"—and other nights behind wheels leading away from the one who became one of the six, blasting away through the night, trailing broken shackles and manacles behind, like the chains ghosts drag through the halls of haunted houses; and nursing a stoned head that would rather leave and learn than stay and stagnate.

Don't let the sound of your own wheels

Make you crazzzz-y-y-y-y-y-yyyy

One thing the great highways provide for the restless spirit is therapy. A 600 mile night or two or three will straighten the kinks out of the least attentive, most scattered and worst psychotic ever to hit the road in a futile quest to get somewhere else but where he is.

And where am I? I ask myself as me and the Eagles and the VW roll down the hill across the Idaho/Nevada border into Jackpot, Nevada, one of the unique communities on earth.

Truly located in the middle of nowhere, Jackpot's reason for existence is the twenty-four-hour gambling, drinking and whoring available to the bored and boring ranching/farming communities of the Magic Valley, only an hour north for a good lead foot with a six-pack, a rifle rack in his GMC pickup, a craziness for dice and cards, a thirst for the honesty of Nevada's drinking outlook and a hard-on the Magic Valley can't appease. A neon firecracker in the middle of the dark desert, Jackpot is a good place to stop for coffee and gas, which I do; and a bad spot for longhairs to hang out, so I don't.

I entered Nevada and gained an hour, and it took a couple of miles after pulling out of the gaudy casino/low brick motel/house trailer/flashing neon sign city of sin in the desert before I can shake the thought that it matters.

I lost ten points just for being in the right place
At exactly the wrong time

Ten points. Ah, the rating scale. Ten on a scale of...what? Ten? A hundred? A thousand? A billion? It probably matters to the statistician, but not to the heart. Losing is losing; and rating it, like all comparisons, only complicates a simple, or at least straightforward, matter. And you don't need a wristwatch to know that bad timing will gum up the works every time. People who pass on blind curves, who aren't home at 8 a.m. when their mate phones from out-of-town, who have an excessive delay between brain impulse and body reaction, who hit the Bay Bridge at 5 p.m., and who laugh without meaning it and cry without knowing why all suffer from bad timing. People with bad timing are like cars with the same problem: unless it is set right, they burn up and break down and strand you on the highway. This calls to mind an old Hemingway poem:

"I know that monks masturbate at night

And that pet cats screw.

And, yet, what can I do

To set things right?"

Nothing, Ernie, good old master of the pen, and hard liver, who taught us much; you already blew it all over the wall of your Ketchum home, along with your brains and the rest of the top of your head. You made the wrong move that time, old boy; but we love you as much as always, and what you left behind is as good as ever. It stands up to the test, just like you knew it would. Still, I can't help but wish you hadn't blown your brains out. Even though you probably felt like it, you didn't take that trip alone, you know; and, at least at one point, we all know you knew it—each man really is a part of the main, and the bell really does toll for thee. Thee and me. And all the others, too. I love you, man, but you shouldn't forget things like that— even though we all understand the ever-present temptation— because it's WRONG and someone has to clean up the mess left behind. And because that path to death raises inescapable questions about life, and your life in particular, that you didn't answer before cutting out.

LITERARY, PERSONAL MONOLOGUES of the lonely night-time desert highway. The little people's wagon of Germany approaches Contact, Nevada, an amazing oasis of that part of the world; and a different sort of literary memory rolls into the vision of my headlight-consciousness—the time the good but now defunct literary magazine, Contact, tried to buy the city of Contact. My old buddy Nick Cox, of Mill Valley, Reno and Sun Valley, was in on that one. A bunch of writers, artists, publishers, editors, girlfriends, boyfriends, hangers-around, a San Francisco Chronicle reporter and anybody else who could get on the trip, hired a Greyhound bus in Sausalito, where Contact was published, for a well-publicized, three-day bash to Contact, with stops in such classic places as Winnemucca and Elko to check out the whorehouses, casinos, and other local color.

Nevada, one of the more insular states of the Union, had never seen anything quite like it. By the time Contact's Greyhound rolled into Contact, every citizen for a hundred miles around was aware that a bunch of San Francisco perverts, artists, writers, degenerates and weirdoes was going to try to take over the area and set up an artist's colony, where writers could write, painters could paint, potters could pot, sculptors could sculpt and anyone else who had something he wanted to do could do it in peace, quiet (it is very quiet in that part of Nevada) and, more to the point of the whole venture, financial security. Contact planned to take advantage of the money-making opportunities of Nevada's unique gambling, drinking and prostitution laws. They were going to buy Contact, set up a casino, open all-night bars and a whorehouse to finance, not only Contact—which, sadly, expired soon after—but also a Contact colony of artists, writers and all those others who work on the fringes of society, and who, unless they be blessed (cursed?) with genius, usually have a hell of a hard life.

Nevada, however, is a funny place. The Mafia is welcome there. Howard Hughes is welcome. Jimmy the Greek is welcome. But Nevada—a center for John Birch activity, the only state in the Union to elect, in the November 1974 elections, a Republican to a Watergate-tainted Congress, a Republican who ran on a law and order platform—this Nevada wasn't going to have a bunch of artists, faggots, bohemians, perverts, bums and weirdoes living off booze, dice and whores, though, God knows, everybody else in the state does. So Contact and Contact never made contact; but it must have been a good bus ride, as bus rides go; and I think about it and wonder what Nick is up to as Contact passes by for the uncountable time.

And I found out a long time ago
What a woman can do to your soul.
Oh, but she can't take you any way,
You don't already know how to go.

Ah, that line hurts. The truth always cuts close, gets in there and clears out the cobwebs. If she takes you to your knees, to your belly, to the gutter or, on the other half of the eternal arc that will eternally meet itself, if she takes you to your heart, to the stars, to the clear, white light itself, you already know how to get there. Since Adam there have been imitators, innovators and illusionists, but there have been no pioneers in that field. Truth keeps the field clean. We've already been there. On the other hand, each man is his own pioneer, innovator, imitator, deceiver and betrayer. But then again....

God, and I'm not even to Wells. I drink some coffee and eat two ginseng capsules and put a piece of the root under my tongue to dissolve it gradually, and I push the chicken-shit little engine past its break-in limit until I catch myself. What I need, want and truly could use is a real machine—a respectable 150-mph Jaguar or, dream of dreams, one of those vehicles with an Italian name I can never remember that has a 200-mph gauge. Or 300. 400. 500. 600. I don't care. I'd like the feeling of stretching it out to that point where it almost breaks. I mean, give me something I can grab hold of with my mind, something tenuous, tentative and scary. Anything except this goddamn VW that can only move 45 mph, that blackmails you with the explosion of $450 of recent investment and a long night in the Nevada desert and a lot of inconvenience getting to the plane for Argentina, if you aren't a good boy.

So, you know, I'm a good boy. Can't fight blackmail. Especially in a chugging VW creeping through the eternal night that stretches along Nevada's roads until, I have faith, the day will dawn, the light will come, the sun will shine and someday, somewhere, somehow, I'll be able to stop, at least for a while.

Open up your eyes
take the devil from your mind
he's been holding on to you
and you're so hard to find

Yes...yes, indeed...that's why some of the good ones, the friends, the ones of warm embrace and solid handshake and straight, clear talking through the night 'til dawn have been lost along the road.

the wind outside is cold
restless feeling in my soul
tempting me to get away
but there's no place a man can go

No place except on down the road. To California or Argentina or Egypt. Tibet. Mecca. Jerusalem. The Gobi Desert. Easter Island. Or Mount Everest. But there's no place a man can go to get away from himself. The man always has to live with himself. Gotta live with the devil, too, 'cause he's always around. And the first time you forget he's lurking under your nose at the back door, he'll take over your mind and anything else he can get into. The devil's a tricky devil, and the trick is to fight the fucker without hating. It's almost like a game. Yea. And God's always around too, but don't try to play games with God or he'll give you a little bonk on the bean or soul or heart with his forging hammer to put you back line with the universe. It's a contradiction, but, then, what isn't? Just don't play games with THE GAME. If you do, you'll wind up cold and restless and with no place to go.

Jesus, the places the mind goes. I pull into Wells; back in the main artery, pumping cars, trucks, buses, motorcycles and their contents back and forth from coast to coast. At last, in the mainstream. The slight rush from this knowledge is enough, I feel, to insure safe arrival in Elko. I pass through Wells, paying homage and respect to those other times and people and experiences connected with Wells; and, with half-mast eyes, mourning I know not what—yet—I steer on toward the Nevada metropolis of Elko, and I am so tired that I can barely believe it. But I do, anyway. After all, what's the alternative? Belief or death. Quit believing in life and you'll learn to believe in death, for the mind believes what it has knowledge of, while the heart believes in its own experience of the never-ending pumping of lifeblood from womb to tomb—no matter what. You can always trust your own heart; it tells you what is happening. If the heart is peaceful everything's okay. If the heart is troubled or hurting, better find out why. If you can't feel your heart it's time to slow down and learn the subtle, ancient art of feeling. People who take their bearings from the heart are seldom rich or famous, but they are usually happy. The mind, however, is a trickster, addicted to complexity; it only works properly in the universe in conjunction with the heart. Left to its own devices, without the tempering effects of the heart's warmth, the mind can be as cold-blooded, efficient and uncaring as the most advanced, complex, versatile space computer that could ever be made of metal and glass and electrical impulses.

HAL 9000, the computer in the movie 2001 A Space Odyssey was as power-tripping crazy as Goebbels, Genghis Khan, Napoleon, Cortez, Stalin, Hitler, Haldeman, Nixon, J.E. Hoover and the incomparable Richard J. Daley, and HAL was probably a lot more intelligent than any of them, but at least HAL had the excuse of lacking a flesh-and-blood heart pumping its lifeblood through the entire, feeling system. When HAL flipped out it didn't have the safety valve of feeling to temper the abstraction of pure idea. Those other crazy fuckers must have Jacuzzi pumps for hearts, ice water for blood and cement for brains.

Speaking of cement, how much cement, asphalt, rock and brick has been laid in strips around this old world, so me and my brothers and sisters can move about with an ease that would be astonishing were it not so hard? What has mankind really accomplished by using the internal combustion engine, the wheel, the wing and the sail for getting away from himself? I know I've been a few places, and there're a few others I don't yet but almost inescapably will know. And there are others I will never see.

But so what? We've been all the way to the moon, that negative, dead orb that man has somehow romanticized, lionized and instilled with a meaning it does not possess—the

moon has the power of a dead weight, pulling tides and imagination around the earth in rushing waves of energy, but the
moon is only a mirror, reflecting the sun and man's illusions,
just like the mirror on the bathroom wall that man so dearly
loves to gaze upon. Yes, we have been to this moon in our sky,
and all we learned from an enormous waste of thought and
energy and material and resource was what the most ancient
knowledge, the clearest thinkers and the most spiritual
beings have always taught us: our place is earth, our business is
at home, and if we can't take care of it at home, sure as the shit
passed off by politicians as government, we ain't going to take
care of it over at our neighbor's neighbors' place, the moon.

Oh Christ, and here I am again coming back from the
moon, across the great Nevada flats to the Sierra, my home, and
to the burgeoning town of Reno in mountain shadow where I
first came into this world and from where I first saw the Sierra,
and to where I have been continually drawn back from every
tangent I have ever embarked upon. And I was reminded for
the uncountable time that home is in the Sierra and Reno and
the deserts and hills of Nevada, and it even extends down
to the Pacific Ocean and a few places like Berkeley and San
Francisco and Santa Cruz. And there is part of home in Sun
Valley and Aspen, still within my land. And it came to me what
the mourning was, going on inside of me—home was not in
Jackson, and never had been and never could be, though I had
tried to find it there. Oh yes, but trying to make a home where

you do not belong is like trying to find peace of mind on the moon.

One says she's a friend of mine

Ah, yes. Where are you friend? In the Sierra? Certainly not in Jackson. No. Not in Jackson. And the mourning started to break into sadness and the beginning of a new work on a new spiral of an old road. And the changes would not be completed easily or quickly, but they would be made.

Suddenly Elko was upon me. The great starlit night showed the outlines of the fine Ruby Mountains on the left, and the neon glare that was Elko came like a fart in a small room of meditators. I stopped for gas and coffee, to stretch and urinate and to pay silent respects to a couple of friends in town. And I hit the road again, deadly tired, completely grossed-out to discover that my brand-new VW engine that I had been babying through the night had to be pushed to get it to start. $450 and the beast had to be pushed after less than five hundred miles. About a dollar a mile, plus gas and oil. Not too good. Well, what can you expect from a machine? Of all the hundreds of cars, pick-ups, trucks and vans I've owned, borrowed and driven around this world, only two of them had any lasting character: the 1930 Model-A panel truck that my father bought me on my sixteenth birthday for $100—my first vehicle, which I painted blue and silver and installed with a beer-cooler and bed, moved well over 60 mph; it saw me through many fine adventures and nights of the sixteen-year-old road.

And then my present favorite, a 1938 Chevrolet four-speed pick-up with well-worn redwood camper that has, for the past two years, been my consistent home, reliable transportation, conversation piece, haven during peaceful and together times and friend during alone times. All the others are just machines, barely remembered and nearly indistinguishable.

When you push through the night, down the endless meandering highways of the spiraling human mind, the difference between a new Mercedes Benz and a springless dump truck loaded with sheep shit is of secondary importance. Somewhere back there in the darkness I have not the discipline to remember is the pony-express rider, the gypsy, the desert caravan which moves by cool night and sleeps through blistering day, the night raid, and the nighttime walking dreamer. All on the same road.

And why? Almost back to Reno once again, and still asking why. Not to stay, for in a few days more I'll be in Argentina. And I've been there before, too. And I'll return from South America and pass over the Sierra and through Reno and on to Jackson from which I will eventually leave and move back to the Sierra. And I already know it, and isn't that strange? The whole road is strange. And wonderful.

Saroyan once took the words 'voyage' and 'world' and combined them into what he called The Whole Voyald. And what a lovely, mysterious voyald it is, I mutter to myself as I pour some more coffee into the plastic Thermos lid pinched between my two thighs, being careful not to spill and scald and sterilize. I sip the delicious, sleazy, black liquid and force my ponderous eyes to pay attention to the never-ending, flowing asphalt with the white and yellow lines and the white and red and yellow lights attached to other machines, guided by fellow exhausted travelers passing in the night.

And I am suddenly aware of relief, resignation and resolution filling me, all at the same time, brought all the way up from the all-night driver's fatigue and blues by the clear knowledge that the end of my road is not yet in sight.

> *Take it easy*
> *Take it easy*
> *Don't let the sound of your own wheels*
> *Drive you craz-z-z-z-y-y-y-y-y-y-yyyyyy*

Dick Dorworth

Reviews & Reactions

Dorworth is one of the few people who has been there, done that, and lived to write about it. His life is the kind of legend you hear around a campfire. His is a combination of bare-knuckled honesty and a wonderment of why, and how, did he do that?

—Warren Miller, legendary skier and ski movie maker

Easily comparable with Kerouac's *On the Road* and *The Dharma Bums, Night Driving* encompasses far more terrain—geographical, physical, and spiritual.... Any page of this book may change your life.

—Karen Chamberlain, award winning poet and author of *Desert of the Heart: Sojourn in a Community of Solitudes*

Dorworth has a voice, a style, a perspective, a body of knowledge, and most importantly, a passion for his subject matter like no other mountain dwelling, mountain loving writer. I'm not even a skier or a climber (Dorworth is an expert at both) and I still love immersing myself in his words. Above and beyond all else, Dorworth is a master story-teller and, in my world, there is no higher praise.

—M. John Fayhee, editor, *Mountain Gazette*

What Dorworth delivers is connectedness to all things living, and to all things being conceived. A timid explorer myself, by comparison, I always wanted to know whether the adventurers of his era would live long enough to slow down and reflect. Dorworth nails the reflection part, for he treats us to the distilled liquor, the essence, of the craziest and most creative mountain-sized generation that is still (mostly) alive.

—Broughton Coburn, bestselling author of *Everest, Mountain Without Mercy*

Other Books By Dick Dorworth

from Western Eye Press

www.westerneyepress.com

THE PERFECT TURN

and other tales of skiing and skiers

THE STRAIGHT COURSE

speed skiing in the sixties

Like this book, these other titles are also available as
eBooks, in both Kindle and iBook formats,
from amazon.com and Apple's iBookstore.

You can read more from Dick Dorworth
on his blog and web site at:
www.DickDorworth.com

Dick welcomes your feedback.
You can write him
through his blog.

Made in the USA
San Bernardino, CA
30 May 2016